EVERY DAY'S A HOLIDAY

EVERY DAY'S A HOLIDAY

Year-Round Crafting with Kids

by **Heidi Kenney**

photographs by **France Ruffenach**

CHRONICLE BOOKS

SAN FRANCISCO

**For my three boys,
T, K, and B.**

Library of Congress Cataloging-in-Publication
Data available.

ISBN 978-0-8118-7144-0

Manufactured in China

Designed by Jennifer Tolo Pierce
Styling by Ethel Brennan
The photographer wishes to thank all my great little models,
Ethel Brennan for her perfect sense of style, and Amy Treadwell
and Jennifer Tolo Pierce at Chronicle Books for all their
guidance and support.

1 3 5 7 9 10 8 6 4 2

Chronicle Books LLC
680 Second Street
San Francisco, California 94107
www.chroniclebooks.com

CONTENTS

SEED-KEEPER POUCH 47
JOHNNY APPLESEED DAY

MAR 11: small, simple drawstring stamped with apple halves. Use the bag to hold seeds for planting just like the legend of Johnny Appleseed

ERIN GO BRAGH LEPRECHAUN PIN 49
ST. PATRICK'S DAY NO ADULT NEEDED

MAR 17: a leprechaun pin from spun cotton, pipe cleaners, and felt

RECYCLED CARDBOARD FLOWERS 53
SPRING EQUINOX NO ADULT NEEDED

USUALLY MAR 20 OR 21: reuse cardboard cereal or crackers boxes for a flower garden of magnets

April

FAUX CUPCAKES 56
APRIL FOOL'S DAY

APR 1: beautiful faux cupcakes using Styrofoam balls, cupcake liners, and wall putty, perfect for displaying your favorite toppers or vintage cupcake picks

LOVE YOUR MOTHER EARTH TOTE BAG 59
EARTH DAY

APR 22: an easy reusable shopping bag with freezer paper stencils in the shape of planet Earth

PINECONE CHEESE BALL 62
ARBOR DAY

LAST FRIDAY IN APR: a cheese ball shaped into a pinecone and covered in sliced almonds

SPARKLY BUNNIES 65
EASTER

SUNDAY AFTER GOOD FRIDAY, IN MAR OR APR: little glittered rabbit head ornaments made from paper clay, wire, glitter, and paper

May

FLOWERY MAY DAY WREATH 70
MAY DAY

MAY 1: a wreath of flower-punched papers and ribbons

VIVA LA PIÑATA! 73
CINCO DE MAYO

MAY 5: a mini, one-of-a-kind piñata using papier-mâché

IN THE GARDEN FENCE 75
MOTHER'S DAY

2ND SUNDAY IN MAY: a mini fenced garden box from wood to hold a small collection of herbs

December

Packaging & Wrapping

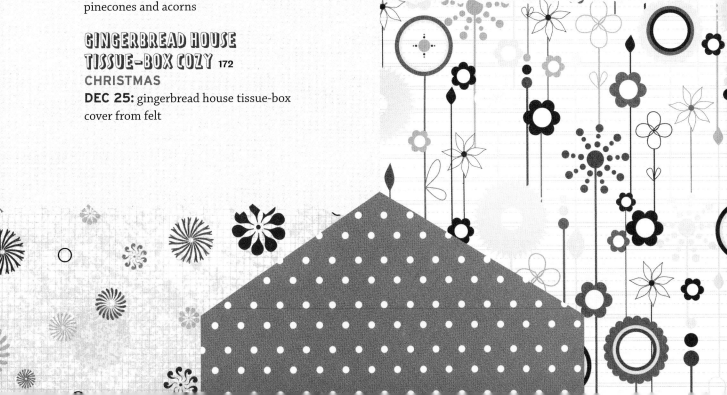

INTRODUCTION

One of my earliest memories of crafting was for Autumnal Equinox. I was in preschool. Using seeds and seed pods, we created little books about autumn and the way the seasons change. This first craft may have been the starting point of my future crafty endeavors. After that came various crafts my mom made with me and my two sisters: cotton-ball chicks for Easter, wiggly-eyed reindeer we assembled from clothespins for Christmas. . . . If a holiday was approaching we were most likely making something at our kitchen table to celebrate it.

Both my parents were creative and understood a child's urge to make things, so we always seemed to have endless supplies on hand: bottles of glue, scraps of fabric, paints, and a sewing machine. Mom and Dad usually had their own projects as well. My mom would work on a new quilt while my dad sculpted little men from clay that he would then bake in our toaster oven. The smell of Sculpey dough baking still takes me back to those days.

My urge to make and create has only increased since having children of my own. Children seem to be born with an interest in making things. They have a natural curiosity about how things are created and do not seem to be held back by some of the fears that plague adults.

Ask any kid under the age of five if they are an artist and it seems like they always say "yes." But don't worry if you're not inherently crafty. You do not have to be a creative or crafty person to make things with your kids. The crafts I've included are very simple and you'll find that the directions are really easy to follow. I've also made an effort to keep the necessary materials simple— things you can easily find at your local craft or hardware store.

In the pages of this book you will find projects and crafts to help celebrate holidays all year long. Kids love celebrating even the smallest occasion. Holidays and crafting give us something to look forward to, something exciting to liven up the days, and there's nothing quite as nice as taking the time to sit with your kids and create something.

I have tried to fill the book with a wide variety of celebrations. You may find holidays you've never heard of and ones you may not celebrate. Don't let this hold you back. Learning about different holidays and customs is half the fun. Let the unfamiliar holidays give you a chance to do some research together.

I've included projects that range in skill level and tools needed. The projects are meant for you and your children to work on together. Some steps will be best for adults to manage, while others you may find your kids are

better at than you. Rest assured that there are plenty of projects here that are appropriate for even the youngest members of the family, these are marked with an icon NO ADULT NEEDED .

I've organized the projects sequentially by month, but don't feel hemmed in by this ordering. If you get the urge to sew the felted trees for Arbor Day in March to create a play forest, go for it! Many of the projects can also be changed slightly to work for other holidays, too. For instance, the Halloween pillow covers can be adapted for any time of year. Using the same instructions, you could create different pillow covers for every holiday. Let the book be a guide to create new play rather than a rigid set of instructions. Most important, have fun!

January

MULTICOLORED NEW YEAR'S HAT

NO ADULT NEEDED

Taking a new twist on classic newspaper hats, these party hats will bring lots of color to any NEW YEAR'S EVE celebration. They are simple to make and can be customized in so many ways. Makes 1 hat

YOU WILL NEED

- 1 sheet large newspaper
- Transparent tape
- Scissors
- White glue
- Several sheets of tissue paper in various colors

1 Lay the sheet of newspaper on a clean work surface. Turn the sheet of newspaper so one of the shorter edges is closest to you. Fold the upper edge down to meet the lower edge, making a rectangle. One of the longer sides of the rectangle will now be closest to you.

2 Take each upper corner, left and right and bring them down to meet at the center of the bottom edge of the newspaper. Smooth the creases with your hand to flatten. You now have a triangle shape that will form the actual hat. Place a strip of transparent tape down the center to attach the two folded triangles together.

3 Using scissors, make a 1-inch cut along the crease on each side, starting at the bottom. Lay the hat down, fold the bottom edge on the side facing you up about 1 inch (be sure to include not only the taped piece but also the piece just beneath it), and crease. This forms the hat brim. You may notice the edges of the brim stick out slightly from the triangle shape of the hat. These ends that stick out can be folded back and tucked into the brim. Then flip the hat over and do the same with the other side, folding up the bottom edge on the remaining panel. To help keep the tucked edges firmly in place you can use a piece of tape, or staple the brim. Any staples and tape will be hidden when the hat is decorated. The hat is ready to decorate.

4 Glue a strip of colored tissue paper along the bottom edge of the hat. Make sure it hangs over the edge by about ½ inch. Repeat on the other side. Set aside.

continued . . .

5 While the glue dries, cut colored tissue paper into 3-inch squares. Using your fingers, crumple these pieces into balls. Kids will love creating these little balls.

6 Use the glue to attach the tissue paper balls to the front of the hat in a design of your choosing. Set aside and let dry.

7 Turn the hat over and decorate the back in the same manner, with more tissue paper balls.

8 Using scissors, make vertical cuts, about ½ inch apart, in the strip of tissue paper along the bottom of each side, to create fringe.

NOTE

Double-stick tape is a good option for attaching the fringe to the hat. The balls are best attached with the glue.

NATIONAL BIRD DAY BOOK

NATIONAL BIRD DAY is the perfect time not only to celebrate birds and their vital part in our environment but to also learn more about them. This project creates a bird-watching notebook that is perfect for drawing birds, documenting habits, nests, and the food they eat. You can stretch out the steps of the project over several days or some can be skipped entirely, for example, instead of embroidering the cover, you can draw it instead. Makes 1 book

YOU WILL NEED

- Mat knife
- Ruler
- 5-by-8-in chipboard
- Tailor's chalk or washable embroidery pen
- Two 5-by-6-in piece tight weave solid color fabric
- 4- to 5-in embroidery hoop
- Scissors

- Embroidery floss in various colors, to complement solid color fabric
- Embroidery needle
- Cardboard (optional)
- Yarn (optional)
- Yarn needle (optional)
- Foam brush
- Tacky glue

- 9-by-12-in piece felt
- Paper cutter (optional)
- ½-in stack colored paper (blank colorful paper, pages salvaged from old bird books, lined paper, and pieces of graph paper are all good choices)
- Two ½-in binder clips

1 Using a mat knife and a ruler on a clean work surface, the supervising adult should cut the chipboard into 2 pieces, each measuring 4 by 5 inches. These pieces will be the base for the front and back covers of the notebook.

2 Using tailor's chalk, make a line ½ inch from the edge on all sides of one of the pieces of solid-color fabric. The ½-inch edges will be turned under when you create the book. Let your child draw a bird and write a word or two in the middle of the fabric, keeping in mind the

continued . . .

guidelines—you want the whole design to show after you turn the edges under.

3 Put the fabric into the embroidery hoop: Loosen the screw on the hoop and separate the top ring from the bottom. Place the bottom (smaller) ring down on a flat surface and then lay the fabric on top, with the design side up and the drawing centered in the hoop. Then position the top ring on top of the fabric so both rings meet up. You may have to adjust the screw to loosen the top ring even more until you can slide it down over the bottom ring, with the fabric sandwiched in the middle. Make sure the fabric is taut. Tighten the screw so the whole thing stays together firmly.

4 Using scissors, cut a length of embroidery floss about 12 inches long. Thread the needle, and knot one end of the floss.

5 Next, backstitch the design. Starting from the underside, position the needle along one of the lines in the drawing and insert it into the fabric. Pull the needle all the way through to the front until the knot catches on the fabric. Push the needle down into the fabric about $\frac{1}{16}$ inch away from where it came up, along the line of your design. Pull the needle all the way through to the back until the thread is taut.

6 You now have one stitch. Push the needle up through the back of the fabric about $\frac{1}{16}$ inch farther down the drawn line, and pull it all the way through again. Insert the needle down into the end point of your previous stitch.

NOTE

If embroidery is too difficult for younger children, they can draw the design and the supervising adult or older sibling can stitch it. Meanwhile, feel free to punch holes in a piece of cardboard and give younger kids yarn and a yarn needle so they can practice stitching.

Push the needle up through the back of the fabric $\frac{1}{16}$ inch past the end of the previous stitch, and continue in this way until the outline of your design is complete. You can change colors as needed, always finishing each color with a double knot on the underside, and beginning again, also at the underside, with new floss.

7 Once the outline of the bird and any words are embroidered, knot the thread on the underside and remove the fabric from the hoop.

8 Using a foam brush, spread glue in an even layer on one side of each piece of chipboard.

9 Lay the 2 solid colored fabric pieces facedown on the work surface and then carefully lay the chipboard, glue side down, in the center of each fabric piece. Press firmly. Let dry.

10 Using scissors, cut the felt into a 4-by-11 inch piece. Set aside.

continued . . .

11 Using the foam brush, spread a ½-inch border of glue around the edge of each piece of chipboard. Take the fabric that is sticking out from the edges of the underside and fold it over onto the glue, one side at a time. Fold the fabric at the corners neatly and press down; add an additional thin layer of glue at the corners if necessary. Let dry.

12 Spread an even coat of glue over the back side of each chipboard piece. Be sure to spread glue over the newly folded and glued edges as well.

13 Lay the felt piece on the work surface, and then position the front-cover chipboard piece, glue side down, on top of it. Position this so that the design is **Right** side up, and the bottom edge of the front cover precisely aligns with the bottom 4-inch edge of the felt (see diagrams a and b).

14 Now spin the entire felt piece around so that the book cover is away from you and the blank felt is in front of you. Glue the back-cover chipboard down so the bottom edge precisely aligns with the 4-inch edge of the felt that is near you. There will be a 1-inch wide space on the felt between the covers (see diagrams c and d).

15 Place some heavy books over both covers and allow to dry.

16 Using the paper cutter or scissors, the supervising adult should cut the sheets, a couple at a time, into 3½-by-5-inch pieces. Don't worry if the pages are not perfectly even.

17 Gather the cut pages into a nice tight stack. With both hands around the stack, bang the top of the stack against the work surface a few times to align the top edge (this is

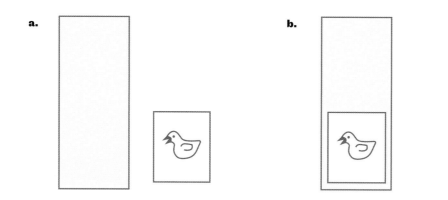

the edge that will be glued to the felt binding of the book). If the stack of pages is slightly uneven on the sides or bottom, that is fine.

18 Using the binder clips, clip each side of the stack to hold it in place. Spread a thick layer of the glue along the top (aligned) edge of the paper stack. Allow it to dry for an hour or so and then spread it with another thick layer of glue.

19 While the glue on the stack is still wet, attach it to the covers. Place the cover piece on the work surface so the felt is facing up. Place the wet end of the pages so that it presses against the center of the exposed 1-inch felt. Close the book. Press down on it a few times to get it nice and tight. Using the binder clips, clip the whole book together and allow it to dry overnight.

20 Cut fun shapes from the extra felt and glue them onto the cover, if you wish. Let dry.

21 Now the book is finished and can be used for bird watching, bird sketching, or writing about our feathered friends.

c.

d.

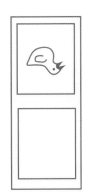

MARTIN LUTHER KING JR. DAY

3RD MONDAY IN JAN

"I HAVE A DREAM" CROSS-STITCH SAMPLER

MARTIN LUTHER KING JR. DAY is celebrated each year to remember Dr. King's important role in the fight for civil rights. In 1963, he gave a speech to more then 250,000 people that was also broadcast on radio and reprinted in magazines and newspapers all over the world. This famous speech is a wonderful way to celebrate Dr. King and his powerful words. Using cross-stitch to create the words, his speech is broken down into small quotes to hang on your wall. Makes 1 sampler

--- YOU WILL NEED ---

- Pencil
- Graph paper
- Aida cloth measuring 3 inches wider and taller than embroidery hoop (see note, page 26)

- Tailor's chalk
- Paint (optional)
- Paintbrush (optional)
- Embroidery hoop
- Embroidery floss in colors contrasting Aida cloth

- Embroidery needle
- Scissors
- Tacky glue
- Felt

1 Start by reading Martin Luther King's famous speech, "I Have a Dream." You'll find it at your local library or online. Go over the language in the speech, talk with your children about what it means, and choose a quote—ideally a shorter one if you and your children are not experienced embroiderers. I chose the speech title for this project.

2 Using a pencil, write the quote on a sheet of graph paper, in an arrangement that will fit neatly in the embroidery hoop. Each square on the graph paper will form one part of each letter. The letters can be as small or as large as you would like.

continued . . .

3 Find the center of the quote. It is sometimes helpful to mark this lightly with a highlighter. Then find the center of the Aida cloth, and make a small mark there with tailor's chalk or make a small stitch in the cloth to remind yourself where the center is.

4 If you like, paint the embroidery hoop, as the finished project will remain in the hoop for display. Sometimes thrift shops have beautiful old metal or colored plastic hoops that make gorgeous displays. If you paint the hoop, take both rings apart first and allow to dry fully before continuing with the project.

5 Put the Aida cloth into the embroidery hoop. Loosen the screw on the hoop and separate the top ring from the bottom. Place the bottom (smaller) ring down on a flat surface and then lay the fabric on top. Then position the top ring on top of the fabric so both rings meet up. You may have to adjust the screw to loosen the top ring even more until you can slide it down over the bottom ring, with the fabric sandwiched in the middle. Make sure the fabric is taut. Tighten the screw so the whole thing stays together firmly.

NOTE

Aida cloth, a fabric made for cross-stitching, comes in a variety of colors and counts (the number of the count indicates the number of holes per inch). For younger children and beginners, fewer holes per inch is easiest.

6 Match up the center marks on the graph paper and cloth. (Keep in mind that each filled-in square on the graph paper will represent one X that you will sew.) Using tailor's chalk, lightly copy the letters from the graph paper onto the Aida cloth.

7 Younger children may need assistance using a needle at this point. Thread a 12 inch length of embroidery floss through the needle, leaving a 2- to 3-inch tail. There is no need to knot the thread. To begin stitching, bring the needle up through the back of the fabric, leaving about a 1-inch tail on the back side. Make the first X in the fabric by going into the hole that is diagonally across and down from the one you came up through, and pulling it taut (be sure to hold the tail). Then, while still holding the tail on the under side, bring the needle back through the cloth, coming up through the hole directly above the hole you went down through. To complete the X, go back in again through the hole that is diagonally across and up from the one you came up through. This creates one small X in the fabric—one part of the first letter.

 8 Once one letter is finished, carry the thread across the back of the cloth to begin the next letter. If the threads show

through (this can happen with Aida cloth that is a light color), you might choose to instead end the thread and begin again for each letter.

9 When all the letters are finished, end the thread by turning the piece over to the **Wrong** side and pushing the needle through the back of a few stitches (without pushing it through to the front). Then tie a small knot to ensure that it will not come undone.

10 To finish the piece so it can be hung on a wall, use scissors to trim the edge of the Aida cloth around the hoop so that only a small amount sticks out. Spread a thin layer of glue around the inside of the embroidery hoop and fold the extra cloth as flat as possible inside the hoop, so it sticks to the glue. Let dry.

11 Cut a circle of felt that is just slightly wider in diameter than the hoop. Press this inside the back of the hoop to cover the back of the stitches.

12 Hang on the wall and be inspired by Dr. King's words whenever you pass it.

February

PUNXSUTAWNEY PHIL SHADOW PUPPET

It is said that Punxsutawney Phil the groundhog comes out of his hole each year on February 2 to look for his shadow. If he sees his shadow it means six more weeks of winter, and if he doesn't it means that spring is on its way. With this project you and your kids can create your own groundhog's shadows to celebrate. **Makes 1 puppet**

YOU WILL NEED

- Scissors
- One 9-by-12-in sheet stiff black paper
- 1/16-in hole punch
- 2 brads
- One 9-by-12-in sheet black construction paper
- Glue
- 1 wooden skewer
- Flashlight

1 Using scissors and following the template on page 183 as a guide, cut the groundhog body parts out of the stiff black paper. The templates can be enlarged or reduced using a photocopier, depending on how big you want the groundhog to be.

2 Punch holes in the body and arms according to the marks on the template.

3 Layer the arms over the body so the holes match up. Put a brad through each set of holes. Now you will have 3 connected pieces that can move.

4 Cut 3 small squares of black construction paper, each about 1 by 1 inch. Put small dabs of glue on the back side of the body. Then lay the end of the wooden skewer down in the glue. Drizzle a little more glue over the end of the wooden skewer and then lay a square of construction paper on top. With your fingers, smooth the paper down so it adheres to the skewer and down onto the stiff black paper. Let dry.

5 Point a flashlight at a blank wall. Hold the groundhog in front of the light to create a large shadow on the wall. Practice making him see his shadow and crawl back into his burrow for six more weeks of winter.

MARDI GRAS MERINGUES

MARDI GRAS means "Fat Tuesday" in French. Mardi Gras celebrations sometimes extend beyond the day before Ash Wednesday, depending on the country, and even between states in the United States. This festive season before Lent, also called Carnival, involves public celebrations, parades, and street parties. No matter how—or how long—you celebrate, you probably think of lots of colors, festivities, and fun when you call Mardi Gras to mind. These colorful meringue cookies are homage to all those brightly dressed costumed people.

Makes about 25 meringues

YOU WILL NEED

- Baking sheet
- Parchment paper
- 3 large eggs
- Large mixing bowl
- Stand mixer or hand mixer
- ½ tsp vanilla

- ¼ tsp cream of tartar
- ¾ cup powdered sugar
- Spoon
- 3 to 6 bowls
- Food coloring in colors of your choice

- 3 to 6 qt-size resealable plastic bags
- Scissors
- ½ cup sprinkles or nonpareils (optional)

NOTE

Meringues are a light airy cookie made with very few ingredients. The baking process can be long, so prepare the kids for the wait. These are great cookies to bake in the morning to be enjoyed in the afternoon. They bake best on dry days, so if you bake them on a humid or rainy day, they may need an extra 30 to 60 minutes in the oven.

1 Preheat an oven to 200°F. Line a baking sheet with parchment paper.

2 First you need to separate the eggs. This can be tricky and is best left to adults or

continued . . .

older kids to do, since if any yolk gets into the whites you will have a difficult time getting the whites to whip properly. Carefully crack each eggshell in half over a large mixing bowl (the mixing bowl for the stand mixer, if using) and open the shell slowly, keeping the intact yolk inside the half shell and letting only the white drip out into the bowl. Carefully move the yolk back and forth a few times between shell halves to get all the white to fall into the bowl.

 3 Once all the whites are in the bowl, add the vanilla and cream of tartar.

4 Beat the mixture on medium to high speed until soft peaks begin to form. This is a magical thing to watch, so be sure the kids are taking part.

5 Slowly add the sugar while still beating the mixture.

6 Beat the mixture until it holds stiff peaks. You can check this by pulling the mixture upward with a spoon and seeing if the whites hold their position.

 7 Divide the mixture among 3 to 6 small bowls, and add 1 or 2 drops of food coloring to each bowl. Blend very gently with a spoon.

 8 Gently scoop the colored mixtures into the bags. If you like, scoop a little of one color into a bag and then add some more of a different color; do not mix the two colors in the bag. If you prefer single-colored cookies, keep one color per bag.

9 Seal, and use a pair of scissors to snip one corner of each bag.

10 Children can squeeze the bags gently to pipe a bit of the fluffy mixture onto the parchment paper–lined baking sheet. Use an upward sweeping motion at the end of each piping to break the meringue mixture off in a peak. They should be 1 to 2 inches wide.

11 Once all of the egg mixture has been piped onto the baking sheet, scatter the sprinkles lightly over the top, if using.

12 Bake the meringues for 1½ to 2 hours. The meringues are done when they are still bright colored (they should not brown) but very crisp. Turn off the oven, open the oven door a few inches, and allow the meringues to dry in the oven for 2 more hours.

FELTED LOVE BUGS

These easy felted love bugs are a wonderful alternative to store-bought valentines. Attach a small note, and you have some memorable valentines for everyone you love. Makes at least 10 bugs

YOU WILL NEED

- ½ to 1 oz red, pink, or purple wool roving
- Nylon pantyhose
- Cotton string
- Washing machine

- 1 tbsp laundry detergent
- Black quilting thread
- Sewing needle
- About 20 small black beads
- Scissors

- White felt scraps
- Tacky glue (optional)

NOTE A running stitch is a straight stitch made by passing the needle through the top and then bottom of the fabric to create a straight line of stitches.

1 Divide the roving into small piles, with 1 pile for each bug. With your hands, shape and roll each pile of roving into a ball shape.

2 Push a small ball far into a leg of the pantyhose.

3 Tie the ball in place at the bottom of the pantyhose leg with the cotton string.

4 Take the next ball and push it far down in the same pantyhose leg. The string you tied above the first ball will keep the two balls from felting together. Using more cotton string, tie the second ball in place (above the first). Repeat until all the balls are stuffed and tied, one on top of the other, in the pantyhose. Tie off at the top with cotton string. You should have what looks a bit like a string of beads, with all the wool roving balls secured inside the pantyhose.

5 Place the hose into a washing machine. Add the detergent and turn on the washer. Use the hottest temperature setting and the

continued . . .

lowest water-level setting (if available) on your washer, and set it for a long cycle. (The agitation helps the fibers adhere to one another, forming a smooth tight ball.)

6 When the washing cycle is done, pull the hose out. Cut away the cotton threads and gently peel the wool balls out of the pantyhose. Roll the balls around in your hands to smooth any loose fibers. They may be slightly bean shaped, but that is fine. Allow them to dry completely.

7 Thread the needle and knot the thread at one end. Sew 2 bead eyes on to each bug, next to each other near one end. Once you determine where you would like your eyes, push your threaded needle into the felt ball where one eye will be, and push it back out through the other eye position. The knot will be hidden once the eyes are in place. Now take one eye and push it onto your needle and down to the felt bug. Push your threaded needle back into the felt body close to where the needle came out, and this time come back out near your knot. Add the second bead to the needle and push your needle back into the head very close to the knot. Then both beads will be pulled tightly against the head. Repeat this step several times going back through each bead until the eyes are firmly attached. Push the needle back out as close to a bead as possible, tie off the end, then cut the extra thread off. Repeat with the rest of the bugs.

8 To make the antenna, thread the needle and insert the needle into the head, just above an eye. Pull the needle through the head and out just above the other eye so there are two strands of threads sticking out of the top of the bug. Using scissors, cut the thread connected to the needle 2 to 3 inches away from the bug. Knot each thread about 1 inch away from the bug and then trim the threads just above the knots. Repeat with the rest of the bugs.

9 Using scissors, cut wings from the white felt using the template on page 185 as a guide. Each bug gets one set of wings sewn or glued into the center of the top of the bug's body. Sew the wings on across the top of the body with just a few running stitches to hold them, or attach them with a few dabs of tacky glue. Repeat with the rest of the bugs.

10 Your love bugs are finished and ready to be delivered to your friends and loved ones.

MINI PRESIDENT FIGURINES

What better way to celebrate PRESIDENTS' DAY than creating mini president figurines? The small wooden bodies can be found at most craft stores.

Makes 4 presidents

YOU WILL NEED

- Small paintbrush
- Acrylic paint (color of presidents' hair and clothing)
- 4 mini wooden figures
- Black fine-point felt-tip pen
- Scissors
- Pipe cleaners in various widths and neutral colors, such as white, gray, brown, and black
- Tacky glue
- Tiny plastic hats, bits of fabric, and other small presidential accessories (optional)

1 Choose the presidents that you'll be re-creating. You may want to print out pictures of your favorites for reference.

2 Using paintbrush and paint, add hair and clothing to the wooden figure. Start with the lightest colors, such as white and light gray (so you can paint over any mistakes with darker colors). Move on to the darker colors. Leave the faces and hands unpainted natural wood. Don't worry about details; you will draw on faces, buttons, and collars with the pen later. Let dry completely.

3 Using the felt-tip pen, let the children add eyes, nose, and mouth to each figure—small dots work perfectly and do not require such a steady hand. The supervising adult may want to tackle outlining the clothing, creating collars, buttons, shirt ruffles, and sleeves. Let dry completely.

4 Using scissors, cut the pipe cleaners to use for hair, sideburns, and beards. Depending on the president you have chosen, cut small pieces of pipe cleaner to use as sideburns or hair curls, and longer pieces to wrap around the face for beards. Pipe cleaners come in many sizes and types, so experiment until you find the one that gives the look you want. Dot small amounts of glue onto the figures, and hold the pipe cleaners in place for about 5 minutes, until dry.

5 Attach small plastic accessories such as Abraham Lincoln's famous black hat using dots of glue. Allow the figures to dry for several hours.

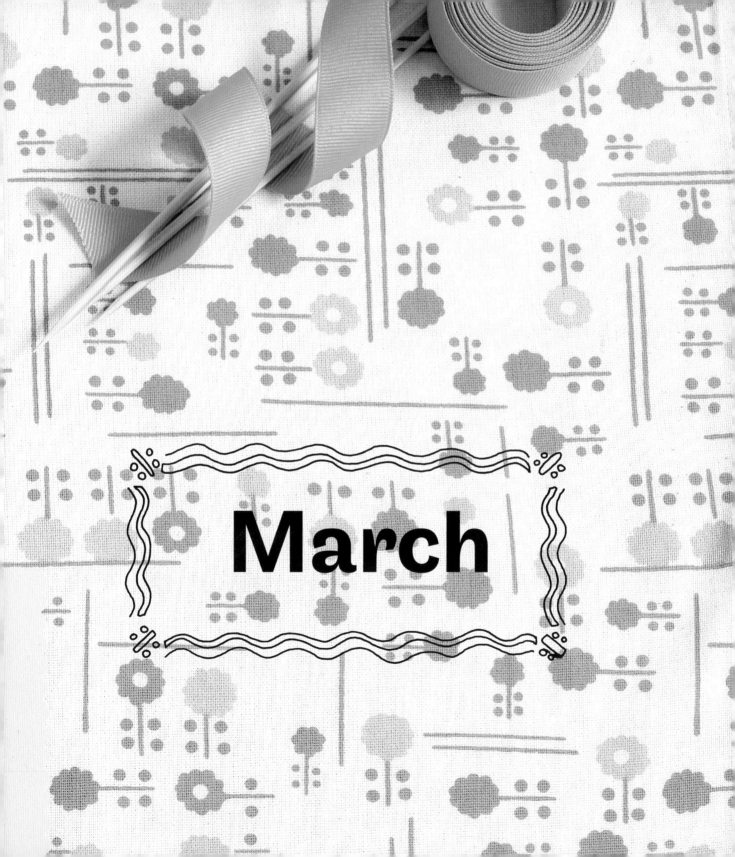

March

PRIZE-WINNING "PI" PIE

Pi is a magic number that has been around for thousands of years. It is an endless number, and worth celebrating. Most people shorten pi to 3.14, which is why PI DAY **is celebrated on March 14. Pi is the number you get when you divide the circumference (the distance around a circle) by its diameter (the distance across a circle at its widest point). In math, pi is written using the Greek letter for "P" and is pronounced "pie." Create these pie-shaped ribbons to wear on Pi Day.** Makes 1 ribbon

YOU WILL NEED

- Scissors
- ⅛ yd light brown or tan felt
- Dark brown embroidery floss
- Embroidery needle

- One 1½-in button-covering kit, available in the notions section of most craft or fabric stores (see note)
- Thread

- Tacky glue
- 1½ yd each ribbon, at least 2 different colors of your choice, ¾ in wide
- Magnet or pin (optional)

NOTE

Some button kits come with teeth around which the fabric wraps; others have a small rubber button maker and pusher that you use to create the button. I prefer the second variety because they are easy to use and don't have any sharp teeth that little fingers can catch on. You can use a different color button center to create different pies. Orange felt makes a great pumpkin pie, and red is good for cherry.

1 Using scissors, cut a circle from the brown felt that is ½ inch larger in diameter than your button.

2 Make 4 small stitches in the center of the felt circle using the embroidery floss and needle to create the slits in the pie's upper crust.

continued ...

These stitches can be made to resemble the letter *X*, with the lines never touching at the center.

3 Using the button-covering kit, line up the felt circle so the slits of the pie are centered over the button. Follow the kit's instructions and cover the button.

4 For the pie's bottom crust (the layer directly beneath the button), cut a piece of felt measuring approximately ½ by 3 inches.

5 Thread your needle with thread or floss. Using a running stitch, make stitches across the strip of pie crust. Keep your stitches to the upper half of the crust, this way the stitches will be hidden later. When you get to the end of the felt, gently pull on the thread or floss. The felt will begin to ruffle and look more like the crust of a pie. Pull slowly so you do not break the thread. Continue to pull and ruffle the felt until it forms a circle (see diagrams a and b). Then use a few small running stitches (see note, page 35)

to stitch the circle closed. You will be sewing one end of the crust to the other to hold it in this circular position. Then knot the thread and clip off any excess.

6 Apply tacky glue to the back of the button, and press the button onto the ruffled crust. The crust's ruffles should stick out around the edge of the button. Let dry.

7 Using scissors, cut two 8-inch long pieces of ribbon from one of the colors. Take one piece of the cut ribbon and lay it out flat in front of you. While referring to diagrams c, d, and e for guidance, bring each end of the ribbon into the center and glue down in place (each ribbon will make two loops). By gluing the ends of the ribbon to the center line you will have created a looped ribbon piece. Set aside to dry and do the same with the other cut ribbons. Continue the same process with your next ribbon color. You can create as many ribbon layers as you'd like to create a big fluffy bow, but you will need at least 8 looped ribbons.

a.

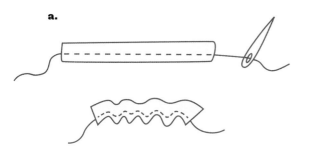

b.

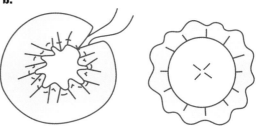

8 Using scissors, cut two 14-inch-long pieces of ribbon from two colors. These will hang down below the pie to look like a real prize ribbon.

9 Take one cut ribbon and fold it in half. Gently pull each end of the folded ribbon so that it fans out on either side from the fold. It will look like an upside down letter V. Apply glue near the fold to hold it in place. Fold and arrange the other color ribbon in the same way, so that each folded ribbon resembles an upside down letter V shape. Apply glue near the fold to hold it in place. Then glue the two ribbons together, arranging them so that the strips that hang down are fanned out evenly and attractively. Let dry.

10 Apply a generous amount of glue to the back of the round bow, and press the folds of the fanned ribbons onto the glue, to attach the two pieces together.

11 Apply a generous amount of glue to the back of the pie and press it down onto the middle of the round bow. Place it on a clean surface, put a weight on top, and let the whole piece dry for several hours.

12 Once the prize ribbon is completely dry, you can glue a strong magnet (for attaching to the refrigerator) or a pin (for wearing) to the back. Or you can attach a thinner ribbon, pulled through the top loop, for hanging.

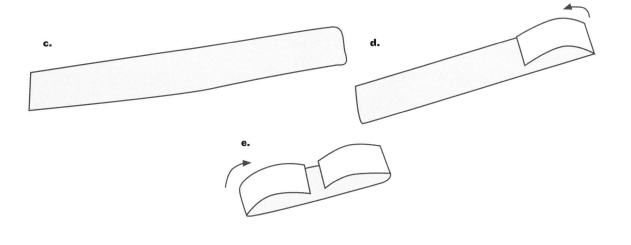

c.

d.

e.

SEED-KEEPER POUCH

Now you can become your own legend just like Johnny Appleseed. He was born as John Chapman and is known for introducing apple trees to large parts of states such as Ohio, Illinois, and Indiana. While he didn't walk around spreading seeds wherever he walked (like the well-known story), he did plants many nurseries of trees that he left in the care of others. Be that as it may, it's still fun to create a seed pouch with your kids, to spread seeds like the legend.

Makes 1 pouch

- **YOU WILL NEED** -

- 8-by-10-in piece muslin
- Pins
- Needle or sewing machine
- Thread to match fabric
- Scissors

- ½ yd cotton cording
- Tape
- Wooden skewer
- 8-by-10-in scrap cardboard (cereal boxes work well)

- 1 apple
- Foam brush
- Acrylic paint in green or red
- Seeds of your choice

1 Lay the muslin on a clean work surface. Fold each of the short edges over ½ inch (this will create the pocket for the cording) and pin down. Using needle and thread or a sewing machine, make a running stitch (see note, page 35) along each short edge, right below the fold, leaving enough room for the cord to slip through.

2 Fold the fabric in half crosswise, **Right** sides together, so the short edges are aligned.

3 Sew up both sides of the bag using a running stitch, about ⅝ inch from the edge, stopping before you reach the cording pocket. Turn the bag **Right** side out.

continued . . .

4 Using scissors, cut the cotton cording in half. This will give you 2 pieces, each ¼ yard long.

5 Using tape, attach one piece of cotton cording to the wooden skewer. Using the skewer will make it easier to put the cording through the pocket. Leaving a tail, feed the cording through the first pocket, around through the second pocket, and out the opening. Tie the ends together in a knot. This is one half of the drawstring.

6 Attach the second piece of cording to the wooden skewer. Follow the instructions in step 5, but start on the opposite side of the bag this time. When you bring the cording through, tie it with the other end. Now the bag will have two drawstrings, one coming out of either side of the bag. When you pull both of these at the same time the bag will close at the top.

7 Slide a scrap of cardboard inside the bag.

8 An adult should cut the apple in half. Children can decide which half to use to stamp the bag.

9 Using the foam brush, brush the paint on the apple half, and practice stamping on scrap paper a few times before you stamp the bag. Once the kids get the hang of stamping, stamp the bag and allow to dry for several hours. Once the bag is dry, remove the cardboard and fill it with seeds, or use it to store extra seeds.

8 inches

10 inches

ERIN GO BRAGH LEPRECHAUN PIN

NO ADULT NEEDED

ST. PATRICK'S DAY is a celebration of all things Irish. You don't have to be Irish to celebrate. Create this little green leprechaun pin to wear all day. Makes 1 pin

YOU WILL NEED

- Glue
- One ³⁄₈-in diameter ball spun cotton (also called "watte" cotton)
- One ³⁄₄-in-tall bell-, oval-, or pear-shaped spun cotton

- Small paintbrush
- Acrylic paint in skin tone
- Scissors
- 4-in square green felt
- 2-in gold rickrack
- 1 black pipe cleaner

- Red and black fine-point felt-tip pens
- 1 tiny black plastic hat (optional)
- One ³⁄₄-in pin back

1 Using the glue, attach the ball-shaped spun cotton to the narrow tip of the bell-, oval-, or pear-shaped spun cotton. The ball will be the head, and the bell will be the body. Let dry.

2 Using the paintbrush, cover the entire head with the paint. Let dry.

3 Using scissors, cut the green felt into 1-by-1½-inch rectangles.

4 Using scissors, cut the gold rickrack to a length that will wrap around the body one time; this will be the belt.

5 Dot the body with dabs of glue, then wrap the green clothing felt around the body. When the clothing is set in place, glue the rickrack around the waist.

6 Using scissors, cut a piece of pipe cleaner to fit the bottom of the leprechaun's face to make a beard. Make a thin line of glue along

continued . . .

the beard line on the face, attach the beard to the glue, and hold in place for several seconds so the glue can get a good grip.

7 Cut 2 legs from the pipe cleaner, long enough to show past the clothing. Bend the ends slightly for feet.

8 Make 2 dots of glue on the bottom of the body, and attach the legs so they stick out from under the felt clothing.

9 Let the younger children create eyes, eyebrows, and a nose with the black felt-tip pen, and a mouth with the red pen.

Small dots work perfectly and do not require such a steady hand. Let dry completely.

10 Attach the hat to the head, if using, with dots of glue.

11 Make a line of glue on the back of the body and attach the pin back. Hold in place for several seconds. Let dry completely.

RECYCLED CARD-BOARD FLOWERS

NO ADULT NEEDED

It's exciting when winter melts away and the warmth of spring begins. But, just because the calendar says its time for spring doesn't mean the days are warm and filled with flowers. This fun flower project made from colorful cardboard boxes brings a flower garden indoors while you wait for the real thing to come. Makes 8 to 10 flowers

YOU WILL NEED

- Scissors
- Cereal boxes or other thin cardboard food boxes in a variety of bright colors,

including green
- Pinking shears or other decorative-edge scissors (optional)

- Tacky glue
- Adhesive-backed magnets or wooden skewers, 1 for each flower

1 Using scissors, cut fanciful flower pieces from the colorful cardboard. Lay out in piles with the same colors grouped together—yellows, oranges, purples, reds, and blues.

2 Using pinking shears or regular scissors, cut out circles 3 to 4 inches in diameter for the back layer of the flowers. These can be petal shaped or any shape you would like your flowers to take. You will need one circle/flower shape for each flower.

3 Create two or three layers with different colors of the cardboard. Always cut the next layer slightly smaller than the layer below it, so you can see all the colors of the flower when it is complete. Do not glue yet, you may still want to move the pieces around and trade them from one flower to the next.

4 Once you are satisfied with your flowers, cut leaves and stems from green cardboard. You can make stems long, fat, short, or tall! Try the stems with different flowers until you are happy with the results.

5 Apply small amounts of tacky glue to each layer, from the top down and assemble the flowers. Glue the stems on last to the back of the flower petals. Let dry completely.

6 Peel the backing off the magnets and stick them to the back of the petals. If you want to be able to push the flowers into flower pots, use a small amount of tape to adhere a wooden skewer to the cardboard stem. Leave about half of the toothpick hanging out from the bottom of the stem.

April

FAUX CUPCAKES

You can fool everyone with these tasty looking cupcakes. They might look good enough to eat, but they're made from Styrofoam balls and wall putty. These cupcakes are for looking pretty only, so make sure no one tries to really eat them. This project is best left to kids who will not be tempted by the realistic look of the faux frosting. They make a great display all year long, and you can even use them to feature some of your favorite cupcake toppers or small toys. Younger children can help glue sprinkles on once the cupcakes have hardened.

Makes 6 faux cupcakes

YOU WILL NEED

- Disposable butter knife
- 10 to 12 oz wall putty (also called Spackle)
- 6 paper cupcake liners
- Six 2½-in Styrofoam balls for standard-sized cupcakes

- Muffin tin for 6 cupcakes
- Disposable bowl
- Food coloring of your choice in various colors (optional)
- Disposable piping kit (optional)

- Cupcake toppers (optional)
- Small paintbrush
- Tacky glue
- Sprinkles
- Acrylic spray sealant

1 Using a disposable butter knife, spread a small amount of wall putty into the bottom of each cupcake liner. Also spread a small amount of the putty all around each ball. Put the liners into the cupcake tin and press a ball into each liner. The cupcake tin will help the cupcakes keep their shape. Let dry for several hours. Remove from the cupcake tin.

2 In a disposable bowl, stir about 1 cup wall putty with several drops of food coloring until combined, to make the faux frosting; if you wish, you can make several colors. Alternatively, you could leave the putty white. *Make sure to remind children that it is not real frosting and should not be eaten no matter how tempting and real it may look.*

continued . . .

3 Using the disposable butter knife, spread the frosting onto the cupcake tops just as you would frost a regular cupcake. Alternatively, use a disposable piping kit, if you like, to pipe decorative shapes and patterns with the frosting.

4 Add cupcake toppers to the cakes. (Do not add sprinkles while the putty is still wet, because the colors will bleed and create a rainbow mess.) Let dry completely—ideally overnight.

5 Using a small paintbrush, apply a small amount of tacky glue over the top of the dried cupcakes. Sprinkle on the sprinkles and allow the glue to dry completely.

6 Take the cupcakes outside and spray with acrylic sealant, to help adhere the sprinkles and add another protective layer to the cupcakes.

7 Arrange the cupcakes on a plate as a beautiful centerpiece, or display in a cake stand. Remind children that the cupcakes are not for eating.

NOTE

These faux cupcakes provide a great way to display a collection of charming cake toppers without worrying about the cupcakes getting old. The cupcakes can also be made in mini size. Just follow the directions but use mini cupcake liners, and smaller Styrofoam balls.

LOVE YOUR MOTHER EARTH TOTE BAG

EARTH DAY is a day set aside to remember how very special our planet is and remind us that we need to take good care of our one and only home. Celebrate this Earth Day by creating a reusable bag with an image of Earth on the front. You can use it for groceries, library books, and more. Makes 1 tote bag

YOU WILL NEED

- Freezer paper
- Black pen
- Cutting mat
- X-Acto knife
- 12-in-square scrap cardboard

- One blank tote bag at least 8-by-8 in
- Iron
- Blue and brown fabric paint
- Foam brush
- Scissors

- White, black, and pink or red felt scraps
- Tacky glue
- Iron

NOTE

You can also transform a logo tote bag that you have at home by using the reverse side for the stencil, or by sewing fabric over the logo and then stenciling on it.

1 Lay the freezer paper with the waxy side down on a clean work surface, and, using the black pen, trace the earth templates on page 186 onto the nonwaxy side of the freezer paper.

2 Lay the freezer paper on a cutting mat. Using an X-Acto knife, the supervising adult should cut out the stencils, taking care to cut out all the areas you want the paint to fill.

3 Put a piece of scrap cardboard inside the bag to protect it from the fabric paint, which may soak through.

4 The supervising adult should iron the first stencil onto the fabric, waxy side down. This will make the round circle of Earth.

5 Let the children fill in the open area with blue fabric paint using the foam brush. Do not remove the stencil yet. Let dry completely.

continued . . .

6 When the paint is dry, gently peel off the first stencil.

7 The supervising adult should iron on the continents stencil, waxy side down.

8 Using the foam brush, let the children fill in the open areas in this stencil with the brown fabric paint. Do not remove the stencil yet. Let dry completely.

9 For the eyes, cut two white circles and two smaller black circles from the felt scraps. Apply a thin layer of glue to the back of the white circles, and adhere them to the Earth image. Apply a thin layer of tacky glue to the black circles, and adhere them on top of the white circles. For the mouth, cut a smile from pink or red felt, and apply a thin layer of glue to the back of mouth and adhere it to the Earth image. Allow the glue to dry before you use the bag.

PINECONE CHEESE BALL

ARBOR DAY is a holiday designated to encourage people to plant trees. This Arbor Day, create a cheese ball snack that looks like it fell down from a tree. It would be great for a tree-planting party, or just celebrating with your own family. Makes 1 cheese ball

- **YOU WILL NEED** -

- Medium bowl
- 8 oz herbed or plain cream cheese, softened
- 1½ cups shredded Cheddar cheese

- Small saucepan
- 1 tbsp olive oil
- 2 tsp grated onion
- 2 tsp minced garlic
- 1 tbsp chopped parsley
- 1 tbsp Worcestershire sauce

- Serving plate
- 1½ cups sliced almonds
- Fresh rosemary sprigs for garnish

- -

1 In a medium-sized bowl, beat the cream cheese with the cheddar cheese until blended.

2 In a small saucepan over medium heat, add the olive oil, and sauté the onion and garlic until tender. Stir in the parsley and Worcestershire sauce and heat just until warmed.

3 Pour the heated mixture into the cheese mixture and stir until well combined.

4 Cover and refrigerate the mixture for at least 2 hours.

5 Remove from the refrigerator and, using your hands, pat it into a pinecone shape. If you like, you can make 1 large or 2 small. Place on a plate with the wider part of the cone as the base.

6 Starting at the top and working downward, apply the sliced almonds to the cone, overlapping each other, to give it a pinecone-like surface.

7 Refrigerate until ready to use. Garnish with sprigs of fresh rosemary and serve.

SPARKLY BUNNIES

One of my favorite holidays in spring is EASTER Sunday. It reminds me of new beginnings, baby animals, flowers, and, of course, Easter baskets. Use Paperclay and glitter to make bunny heads perfect for baskets or decorations for your Easter table. Makes 10 bunnies

YOU WILL NEED

- Scissors
- 20-in 24-gauge malleable wire
- One 16-oz package Paperclay
- Newspapers
- 2 paintbrushes; 1 for paints, and 1 for glue

- Pink, blue, and green acrylic paint
- Glue
- Pink, blue, and green glitter
- Clear acrylic sealer
- One 9-by-12-in sheet cream construction paper

- Package of wiggly eyes
- Ten 1/4-in pom-poms
- 20-in ribbon for hanging in your choice of color

NOTE

It is nice to have something to hang your bunnies on while you work on them. If you have a small wire tree, jewelry rack, or something else you can suspend them on, you will find this helpful.

1 Using scissors cut the wire into ten 2-inch pieces, one for each bunny. Loop the wire by bringing the cut ends together and then twisting those ends, so that it will stay put in the clay.

2 On a clean work surface, divide the clay into 10 equally sized pieces. Take each piece and work it in your hands until it is soft. Then take 1 wire piece and shape the clay around the wire, covering the twisted section and leaving

continued . . .

the loop uncovered at the top. Work it until you have a nice ball shape. Repeat with the remaining clay and wire to make additional bunnies.

3 Suspend the balls of clay, or set them down gently on a clean surface to dry overnight.

4 Cover a clean work surface with newspaper or other protective covering. With the bunnies hanging from something steady, or while holding the wire in your hand, paint the dried balls of clay with acrylic paint. Coat the entire ball with one color of paint. Hang to dry.

5 Using a paintbrush, spread a thin layer of glue all over each head. Then sprinkle glitter over the glue. Match glitter color to the paint color, and shake to remove excess glitter. Let dry for about an hour.

6 An adult should spray each head with clear acrylic sealer. This helps to keep the glitter on the bunnies and off of your hands. Let dry completely.

7 Meanwhile, using scissors, cut 2 ears for each bunny from the construction paper using the template on page 185 as a guide.

8 Using a paintbrush, apply glue around the edge of each ear. Sprinkle with glitter in a color that matches the bunny that will wear the ears. Do not put any glitter past the fold mark, because this part will be used to adhere the ears to the bunny head. Let dry. Then coat the backs with glue and glitter them as well.

9 As in step 6, an adult should spray both sides of each ear with acrylic sealer. This is optional, but it will help keep the glitter from coming off and is especially useful when you are working with tiny flake glitter. Let dry.

10 Apply a dab of glue to the bottom section of the front of each ear, and press the glued section to each head, positioning on either side of the wire loop.

11 Apply glue to the back of the eyes and to the pom-poms, and press onto the bunnies to make faces. Allow the face and ears to dry and then string hanging ribbon through the wire loop.

May

FLOWERY MAY DAY WREATH

MAY DAY is a very old holiday celebrated in many countries. This holiday brings to mind children dancing and singing around the May Pole, the colorful streamers of ribbon, and hanging baskets of flowers on doorknobs. This wreath aims to evoke all those things with colorful ribbons and paper flowers.

Makes 1 wreath

YOU WILL NEED

- One hundred ½-in sequin pins
- Ten to fifteen 12-in ribbons in colors of your choice
- 8½-in diameter foam wreath
- Flower-shaped hole punch
- Decorative paper or newspaper
- Scissors

---

1 Using a sequin pin, attach one end of a ribbon length to the back of the wreath. Begin to wrap the ribbon around the wreath. Wrap until you reach the end of the ribbon, or cut the ribbons shorter and alternate colors and patterns to create a multicolored wreath. Each time you start and stop a ribbon, use the new ribbon to overlap the last one, and use sequin pins to hold the ends in place. When you are finished wrapping, the wreath will be completely covered in ribbon; none of the foam should be visible.

2 Using the flower-shaped hole punch, cut flowers out of the paper. Children really love using the shaped hole punches to punch out the flowers. Let them experiment with different types of paper.

3 Using sequin pins, attach the flower cutouts to the wreath. Concentrate your efforts on filling the front of the wreath. Don't worry about covering the whole wreath with flowers, because the ribbons can show through beneath and around the flowers. Older children can help with the pinning process.

4 Using scissors, cut a piece of ribbon to create a loop for hanging. Attach the ribbon loop to the wreath using sequin pins. Hang the finished wreath indoors or in a covered area outside so the paper flowers will not wilt in the rain.

VIVA LA PIÑATA!

CINCO DE MAYO is a Mexican holiday that means "fifth of May." The holiday commemorates the Mexican army's victory at the Battle of Puebla on May 5, 1862. Many people all over the United States celebrate this day that honors Mexican heritage. Piñatas are one of the many traditions enjoyed during celebrations. It is very easy to create your own piñata to celebrate.

Makes 1 piñata

YOU WILL NEED

- 1 cup flour
- 2 cups water
- 10 to 20 sheets newspaper, plus more for the work surface
- 1 balloon
- Crepe or tissue paper in colors of your choice

- Scissors
- Small, sharp knife
- Large plastic needle
- Cotton string
- Serrated knife
- Glue
- 1 sheet 8½-by-11-in green construction paper

- 1 sheet 8½-by-11-in red construction paper
- 1 sheet 8½-by-11-in white paper
- Paper scraps in various colors
- Wrapped candies

1 In a small saucepan, add the flour and water and stir until combined. The supervising adult should heat the mixture for 3 to 5 minutes, until it just begins to thicken. Remove from heat and pour into a plastic container to cool.

2 While the mixture cools, tear the newspaper into strips. The strips should be about 2 by 2 inches, but they do not need to be exact.

3 Inflate the balloon to about 4 inches diameter and tie it closed. This will be the main part of the piñata.

continued . . .

4 Cover a clean work surface with extra newspaper, because this part can get a little messy.

5 Dip the newspaper strips into the paste mixture, one at a time, and use your fingers to wipe off excess paste. Place wet newspaper strips around the balloon. Repeat until the whole balloon is covered in one layer. Let dry for 15 minutes. Add another layer of papier-mâché, let dry for 15 minutes, and repeat for final layer. Set the piñata to dry on a piece of newspaper. You will be able to tell when it dries because the newspaper will look lighter and be dry to the touch. Turn the piñata once or twice to make sure it dries all over.

6 Using scissors, cut 20 to 30 two-inch lengths of strips 1 to 2 inches wide.

7 Using scissors, make small cuts about halfway across the width of each strip to turn it into fringe. Just make sure you don't cut all the way through the strip.

8 When the piñata is dry, it is time to remove the balloon. While holding onto the knotted balloon tail pop the balloon and use the tail to pull it out of the top of the piñata. Then an adult should use the knife to make two small cuts into the top of the piñata about 3 inches apart from one another. Thread the large plastic needle with the string and pass it through both slits. Tie the string into a loop for hanging.

9 Beginning at the bottom or top of the piñata, apply a line of glue the length of one of the tissue-paper strips. Press a tissue-paper strip onto the glue, leaving the fringed part unattached. Apply another line of glue and tissue-paper strip slightly overlapping the first, but leaving the fringed part unattached. The fringe will hang over the previous strip, hiding the part that is not fringed. Repeat until the whole piñata is covered. Let dry completely.

10 Using the green and red paper for the mouth and the white paper for the teeth, cut out the mouth and teeth using the templates on page 184. Cut eyes in the shape of your choice using the paper scraps. Sandwich the teeth between the green outer mouth and red inner mouth and glue together. Glue the eyes onto the piñata's face.

11 An adult should cut a small flap in the lower back, using a serrated knife. Then the piñata can be filled with candy. This flap can be lifted to get the candy out without ever needing to break open your piñata.

IN THE GARDEN FENCE

MOTHER'S DAY is one day a year set aside to honor our moms and all they do for us. I am sure there any many special moms we all know, plus grandmothers, aunts, and friends who take care of us just like a mother would. Create this little garden-fenced basket for a special mom. You can fill it with small clay pots for herbs, or potted flowers, or it could be used as a gift basket for a batch of homemade muffins. **Makes 1 fence**

YOU WILL NEED

- 8 sets 3¼-in unpainted mini wooden fencing (see note, page 76)
- 7½-in-square block of wood

- 2 paintbrushes
- Acrylic paint
- Wood glue
- Hammer
- 16 to 24 brads

1 On a covered work surface spread out the fence and wood base. Using a paintbrush, cover all the pieces with acrylic paint. Let dry completely, and then apply a second coat of paint. Let dry again. Flip over the fence pieces to paint the other sides in the same manner. Let dry.

2 Take one of the fencing pieces and, using a clean, dry paintbrush, spread a thin layer of wood glue on the side of the wood base. Press the fencing piece against the glue and hold it in place for a few minute while the glue sets. Repeat with the remainder of the fencing pieces, until all the sides are fenced.

continued . . .

3 The supervising adult should nail the fence to the base, using 2 or 3 brads for each fence piece, along the bottom. Repeat for all four sides.

4 Allow the wood glue to dry thoroughly before handling the fence basket.

A POPPY FOR REMEMBRANCE

MEMORIAL DAY is a day to remember all the men and women who have died in service of the United States. One of the most famous poems from war, "In Flanders Field" written by Canadian Lieutenant Colonel John McCrae, talks about poppies. The poppies in the poem have become a symbol of Remembrance Day over the years. Makes 10 poppies

YOU WILL NEED

- Scissors
- ¼-yd-by-40-in red cotton fabric
- Black quilting thread
- Green floral tape
- 5 green pipe cleaners, cut in half

NOTE Using floral tape can seem tricky, but it is actually very easy. The trick is to stretch the tape as you are wrapping it, gently pulling it and keeping it tight. As you stretch the tape, it becomes somewhat sticky and will adhere to itself. If you would like the poppies to have shorter stems for wearing on the lapel, cut each pipe cleaner into four pieces instead of two.

1 Using scissors, cut 4 petals for each poppy from the red fabric using the template on page 185 as a guide.

2 Cut the thread into 3-inch pieces. You will need 4 pieces for each flower.

3 Lay 4 lengths of the thread in a pile and wrap the end of a pipe cleaner around the center of the threads. Twist the pipe cleaner a few times to secure the threads, representing the stamen.

4 Holding the group of stamen, wrap it with floral tape. As you wrap it, pick up one petal and wrap the bottom of it as well. Continue wrapping, adding one petal at a time, overlapping the previous one until you have all 4 petals wrapped with the stamen in the middle.

5 Continue wrapping down the pipe cleaner with the floral tape until the pipe cleaner is completely covered. Tightly wrap the floral tape one last time at the bottom and break off.

June

MINI RADISH MUSHROOMS

Transform radishes into mini mushrooms that look like they stepped out of a fairy tale. These radish mushrooms are a great way to dress up a big salad full of veggies, and what a wonderful way to celebrate this holiday.
Make as many mushrooms as you have radishes.

--------- **YOU WILL NEED** ---------

- Paring knife
- Red-skinned radishes
- Plastic straw
- Scissors

1 The supervising adult should use the knife to draw a shallow groove, or line, crosswise around the center of each radish.

2 Using the line as a guide, and starting from the top of the radish, carve the mushroom's stem. Cut down toward the diameter all around the radish, leaving a center core that will become the stem.

3 Now cut the tip of the exposed radish core off, so the stem of the mushroom has a nice flat bottom. The radish should now resemble a red mushroom with a white stem.

4 Let the children use the straw to make the "polka dots" for the mushroom. Carefully poke the straw into the mushroom cap, without going in too far. As you pull the straw out a little bit of the radish skin should come out, too, leaving behind the white flesh. If the straw begins to bend, using scissors snip off the end and then keep going.

REUSABLE SILHOUETTE COFFEE CUP SLEEVE

FATHER'S DAY **is a time to celebrate the dads in our lives, and how very special they are. This hot drink cozy will keep fingers from burning when drinking coffee or tea, and is also better for the environment than disposable cozies.**

Makes 1 sleeve

YOU WILL NEED

- Lamp
- Tape
- One sheet paper
- Pencil
- Scissors

- Pins
- 5-in-square black wool felt
- 20-in-square wool felt in any color other than black
- Needle

- Black thread
- Embroidery needle
- Embroidery floss in color of your choice
- 4-in self-adhesive Velcro

1 First, make a tracing of your child's silhouette. Shine a lamp on a blank wall and have your child sit sideways so you can see his or her profile in a shadow on the wall.

2 Tape a piece of paper on the wall and trace the shadow in pencil. You can also let your kids try this with your silhouette.

3 Using a photocopier, reduce the traced silhouette so it can fit on the 5-inch square piece of felt. The size of your original will vary depending on how close to the wall your child was sitting.

4 Using scissors, cut out the reduced silhouette and pin it to the black felt. Cut out the silhouette.

5 Using scissors, cut two of the coffee sleeves from the contrasting felt using the template on page 187 as a guide.

6 Lay one of the coffee sleeves on a clean work surface, so that the shorter edge is closest to you. Pin the silhouette in place on the sleeve; it should be centered. Using needle and black thread, sew around the edge to secure the black felt to the sleeve.

continued . . .

7 Put the coffee sleeves together so the edges match up and the silhouette is on the outside. Using an embroidery needle and floss, blanket stitch around the entire edge of the coffee sleeve to attach. To make the blanket stitch refer to the diagram below. Work your stitches from left to right. Begin by bringing your needle to the outer edge of the fabric at point A. Insert your needle back into the fabric at point B. Push your thread through both fabrics in a straight line so it is coming out at point C. Your thread should be behind the needle as it goes through the fabric. Continue to stitch, taking note that point C now becomes point A for the next stitch. The thread will form a nice edging around the fabric. Finish off with a knot and clip threads.

8 Place the two short ends of the felt together so the sleeve forms a ring, with the ends overlapping by 1 inch or so. Pull apart the Velcro. Pin one part of the Velcro on the inside of the felt, about ¼ inch from the edge. Pin the other part of the Velcro on the outside of the felt, at the other end about ¼ inch from the edge. Practice matching up the Velcro to ensure that the pieces are placed properly, and then peel off the backs and adhere the Velcro to the fabric. Let Velcro sit for the time recommended on the packaging once adhered to fabric.

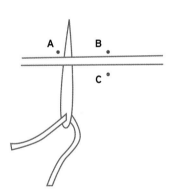

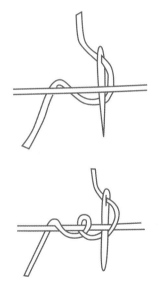

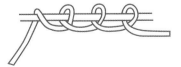

INSECT COLLECTION SHADOW BOX

Insects are a wondrous part of the environment we live in, and a vital one. From the bees that pollinate our flowers to the earth worms that make our soil healthy, insects are amazing. With this project you can create your own display of insects from imaginary to replicas of the real thing, using leaves and flowers arranged in shadow boxes. Makes 1 box

YOU WILL NEED

- Fresh flower petals and leaves, stems, and grass with long stems
- 1 cup vegetable glycerin
- 2 cups hot water
- 4 to 5 glass cups or jars

- Garden shears or a sharp knife
- Paper towels
- Fast-drying acid-free glue pen
- Sequin pins or small straight pins

- Padded shadow box
- White paper (optional)

1 Place the stems in water while you prepare the glycerin.

2 In a large ceramic bowl, stir together the glycerin and hot (not boiling) water until combined. Pour the mixture into the cups or jars, so that each contains about 2 inches of the mixture.

3 The supervising adult should use garden shears or a sharp knife to trim the end of each flower or leaf stem and stick it into the glycerin mixture. The flower will absorb the glycerin, which will preserve it while keeping it soft and pliable. If you have any small petals, leaves, and other small botanical specimens, submerge them in the mixture.

4 Let the flowers and leaves sit in the mixture for about 1 week to preserve.

5 After 1 week, remove the botanical specimens from of the mixture. Allow to air dry on paper towels for 2 more days.

continued . . .

6 Meanwhile, begin researching bugs and insects. Even if you plan to make up your own insects, real specimens can serve as a wonderful source or inspiration. Visit your local library, study pictures of insects, and create sketches of how you'd like your insects to look.

7 Once the flowers are preserved and you are ready to start making bugs, cut the plants into smaller, workable pieces. Study the stems and stamen and notice how they look a lot like legs and bodies. Flower petals make stunning wings, and the backs of beetles can be made from leaves and grass clippings. Play around with the pieces and try different combinations. Assemble the insects.

8 Using a fast-drying acid-free glue pen, glue the pieces of the insects together. Build each insect from the bottom up. Attach the legs to the body, then add wings and antennae, and finally add any wing decorations on top. Make enough insects to be spread across the base of the shadow box with some room between them. Let dry overnight.

9 Using the sequin pins or small straight pins, gently mount each insect to the bottom of the padded shadow box. If you wish, create small labels with white paper to post in the box below each insect.

MARZIPAN DOUGHNUTS

DOUGHNUT DAY celebrates those round treats that come in so very many flavors. Doughnuts may have begun as "oiley cakes" in Holland, and are thought to have gotten their hole in the United States. There is much about doughnut history that is unknown, but they are tasty treats worth celebrating. These mini doughnuts are made from marzipan, a candy treat made of ground almonds. Marzipan works like a clay, making these mini doughnuts fun to make, and without any need for hot oil. Makes 20 to 25 doughnuts

YOU WILL NEED

- 6 to 8 oz marzipan
- Small glass bowl
- Rubber gloves
- Liquid food coloring or gel paste in colors of your choice

- Toothpicks
- Plastic wrap
- Plastic straw
- Small rolling pin
- Parchment paper
- Mini flower–shaped cookie cutter

- Small saucepan
- 2 tbsp light corn syrup
- ¼ cup water
- Pastry brush
- Sprinkles and nonpareils

1 Place ¼ cup marzipan in a small glass bowl (cover the rest while you work, as it can dry out). This will be the original base coloring for the doughnuts. Set aside.

2 Divide the rest of the marzipan into at least three equal parts. The amounts depend on how many colors you want to use for the frosting. While wearing rubber gloves

take one section of marzipan and add 2 drops of food coloring. If using the gel, use a toothpick to add 1 small drop to the marzipan. Knead the dough until the color is mixed through, cover with plastic wrap, and set aside. Repeat with the remaining two marzipan sections and food coloring (other colors, if you like). Keep the marzipan covered while you work.

continued . . .

3 On a flat surface, take a small chunk of the original-colored marzipan from the bowl and roll it into a ball. Press the top slightly to give it that doughnut look, then use the straw to poke out the middle. Repeat, making several doughnuts, always placing them under plastic wrap.

4 Using the rolling pin, roll the food-colored marzipan on parchment paper till about ⅛ inch thick.

5 Using the flower-shaped cookie cutter, cut out frosting, one flower for each doughnut. Use the straw to cut out the middles, and then lay one frosting flower on top of each bare doughnut. Cover each with plastic wrap.

6 In a small saucepan, bring the corn syrup and water to a boil and stir for a few minutes until the syrup dissolves. Remove from heat and let cool.

7 Using a pastry brush, lightly brush glaze on the tops of the doughnuts to which you would like to add sprinkles. Then scatter the sprinkles on top. Let dry uncovered on wax paper for several hours, until the glaze is no longer tacky.

8 Store doughnuts in an airtight container in the refrigerator for up to 1 week.

July

POSTAGE STAMP DAY

JUL 1

SNAIL MAIL STAMPS

NO ADULT NEEDED

POSTAGE STAMP DAY is a great excuse to send mail. With the age of e-mail, sometimes snail mail can seem like a lost art. Turn thumbprints into snail-mail postage stickers to decorate your envelopes, and then send someone you love some mail. *Makes up to 56 standard-size stamps*

YOU WILL NEED

- Ruler
- Pencil
- One 8½-by-10 in sticky-back paper or sheet of labels
- Decorative-edge scissors
- Stamp pad in any color
- Black fine-point felt-tip pen

---

1 Using the ruler and pencil, create a grid of cutting lines for the stamps on the wrong side of the sticky-back paper. Standard stamps measure $^7/_8$ by 1 inch, but you can make your stamp stickers any size you'd like.

2 Using decorative-edge scissors, cut along the cutting lines.

3 Lay out the stamps on a clean work surface. Press your thumb down on the stamp pad to ink it. Press your thumb horizontally onto the center of a stamp to create the shell shape. Repeat with the rest of the stamps, switching to different colors as you wish. Let dry completely.

4 Using the felt-tip pen, draw a swirl over the thumbprint to complete the shell. Start in the center of the thumbprint and use your pen to draw a spiraling circle from this center point to the outer edge of the thumbprint. Draw a small head peeking out of the shell on one end, and a little pointy tail coming out the other side. Add a little smile and a dot for the eye. Draw a pair of antennae coming off the head to finish. Repeat with the rest of the stamps.

5 Using the felt-tip pen, write "snail" above the snail, and "mail" below, or in another position, if you prefer.

6 Peel the backs off of the stickers and use them to decorate mail for a friend. Don't forget to use a real postage stamp for mailing.

CANADA DAY
JUL 1

CANADIAN FLAG GARLAND

CANADA DAY is Canada's national holiday, which celebrates the enactment of the British North America Act of 1867, which united Canada as a single country of four provinces. It is also sometimes called Canada's birthday, so with these homemade flag banners everyone can celebrate. Makes 1 garland

- - - - - - - - - - - - - - - - **YOU WILL NEED** - - - - - - - - - - - - - - - -

- Scissors
- Two 3-by-5-in Styrofoam trays, usually found in the fruit or meat section at grocery shops
- Ruler
- Paper

- Ballpoint pen or wooden skewer
- Glue
- 4-by-7 ¼-in wood block
- 1-yd-by-40-in white felt
- Stack of newspapers

- Red fabric paint
- Ink roller
- 1 to 2 packages white rickrack
- No-sew adhesive glue

1 Using scissors, cut the sides off one Styrofoam tray so that it is a flat surface.

2 Measure and cut two rectangles from one edge of the tray, each measuring 1½ by 4 inches.

3 Using the template on page 185 as a guide, trace the maple leaf onto paper and cut out. Place the maple leaf cutout on the remaining part of the tray and, using a ballpoint pen, draw around it. The maple leaf should be about 3 inches tall.

4 Remove the paper pattern and, using scissors, cut the leaf out.

5 Apply glue to the back sides of the Styrofoam rectangles and maple leaf and press them down on your wooden block, with one stripe on each end and the maple leaf in the middle. It should already begin to resemble the Canadian flag. Let dry.

6 Meanwhile, using scissors, cut rectangles, each 4 by 7 ¼ inches, from the felt. Cut as many as you would like to be in the banner; the

continued . . .

more rectangles you cut, the longer the banner can be.

 7 On the stack of newspapers lay your first blank flag.

8 Squeeze out some fabric paint into the other Styrofoam tray. Coat the roller and roll it around several times in the paint until the paint is spread evenly. Roll the paint-covered roller back and forth across your stamp until the raised parts are evenly coated.

9 Carefully turn the stamp over, line up its corners with those of a blank flag, and press down on to the felt. When you lift it up again you may have to carefully peel your flag off of the stamp. Don't worry if there are any light spots; when all the flags are assembled together they will look wonderful, and small light areas will not be noticed.

10 Lay the stamped flag aside to dry. Repeat until all of the flags are printed. Let the flags dry.

 11 Unfold the rickrack and apply a small layer of adhesive, about 3 inches long. Then press the short edge of one flag onto the adhesive. Work along the rickrack, applying adhesive and flags 2 or 3 inches apart and pressing down with your hands. Let dry completely.

12 Hang your flag banner indoors.

INDEPENDENCE DAY

JUL 4

FOURTH OF JULY SPARKLER

NO ADULT NEEDED

When you think of party poppers you probably think of New Year's Eve. But there's no reason you can't enjoy the fun of poppers in the heat of July. These poppers look like firecrackers and would make great favors for an Independence Day party, or just a little something special at the end of a summer meal.

Makes 3 poppers

- YOU WILL NEED -

- 3 large sheets red tissue paper
- Scissors

- 3 empty toilet paper tubes
- Candy, small trinkets, confetti, stickers, or other goodies to fill the poppers

- Gold or silver pipe cleaners
- Black masking tape or duct tape

 1 Place the 3 sheets of red tissue paper in a stack and, using scissors, cut into 15-inch squares.

2 Stand each empty toilet paper tube in the center of one square of tissue paper.

3 Fill each tube with a small amount of candy, tiny toys, confetti, stickers, or other small treats. Gently bring the tissue paper up around the tube, using one hand to hold the tube and the other to gather and smooth the tissue

paper. Flatten it against the tube; some parts of the tissue paper will fold and overlap.

4 Using scissors, cut a piece of pipe cleaner measuring about 5 inches. To create the sparkler end of the firecracker, cut two more pieces of pipe cleaner measuring about 2 inches long. Twist these 2-inch pieces around the tip of your 5-inch piece. Gently slide the pipe cleaner into the center of your gathered paper so it sticks out about 3 inches with the sparkler end at the top.

continued . . .

5 Now that you have the tissue paper gathered around the top, twist the paper around the pipe cleaner so it begins to form the wick part of the firecracker. You can rub the twisted paper between your two palms to help smooth it; just take it slow so the paper wrapped around the tube does not rip.

6 Cut a 10-inch strip of tape and slowly wrap it around the wick, beginning at the bottom of the wick and working upward. As you wrap, pull the tape tight to smooth the tissue paper even tighter around the pipe cleaner.

7 Stop wrapping with tape just when you get to the sparkler part of the pipe cleaner. Wrap the tape around itself several times to make sure it is secure.

8 To "pop" your firecracker, hold with one hand on the bottom and pull firmly on the wick with your other hand. The tissue paper will rip open to reveal the treats inside.

COOL ICE-CREAM PUPPET

In the heat of summer nothing is quite cooling as ice cream. With this ice-cream puppet you do not have to worry about drippy cones, or a melty mess. A little friend is hidden inside the puppet disguised as a cool summer treat.

Makes 1 puppet

YOU WILL NEED

- Scissors
- ¼-yd-by-40-in solid color polar fleece
- Needle

- Thread in color that coordinates with fabric
- Sewing machine (optional)
- Felt scraps, for puppet face
- Fabric glue
- 15-in dowel rod

- 2 large red wooden beads
- Empty thread cone, or cardboard craft cone
- ¼-yd-by-40-in tan felt

---

1 Using the pattern below as a guide, cut out two ice-cream shapes from the polar fleece fabric.

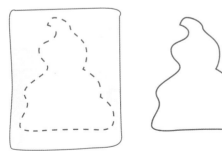

2 Lay the two fabric pieces on a clean work surface, **Right** sides together. Using a needle and thread, or a sewing machine, if you like, sew a running stitch (see note, page 35) about ⅝ inch from the edges of both sides. Turn **Right** side out.

continued . . .

3 Create a face on one side of the ice cream fabric from the felt scraps. Adhere the face to the lower section of the fabric with fabric glue, so that when the puppet is in use the face can be hidden down inside the cone. Allow the glue to dry.

4 Take the dowel and insert it into the unsewn wide opening at the bottom of the polar fleece fabric. The fabric will drape down over the rod looking almost like a dress. Push one red bead down onto the dowel rod so the polar fleece fabric is sandwiched between the two. The bead looks like a cherry on top of the ice cream, and will keep the puppet secured to the dowel rod.

5 Using the diagram below as a guide, cut the cone covering from the tan felt. If the felt is too small or too large for your cone, cut less or more felt to fit. You can create lines on your cone by using a running stitch with needle and thread, or on a sewing machine. The lines should crisscross to appear like a real cone.

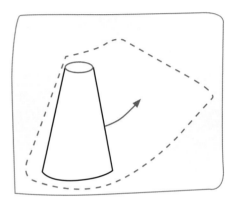

6 Now take the dowel rod and slide the cone up over the bottom, so it meets up with the ice cream fabric. Apply a small line of glue around the outer edge of the cone, and adhere the end of the ice cream to the cone. Allow to dry.

7 Apply glue to the outside of the cone and wrap the tan felt piece around the cone so that the edges overlap by about ½ inch and the cone is completely covered. Press in place until the felt is set. The felt cone should be overlapping the edge of the ice cream fabric so it looks like a real cone of ice cream.

8 Next apply a small amount of glue to the bottom end of the dowel rod and push the final red bead onto the end. This bead helps ensure that the dowel rod will not slide up into the puppet.

9 Once everything is dry you can move the puppet up and down. It will appear to be a normal cone of ice cream until you push the puppet up and reveal the face.

August & September

WATERMELON MONSTER

This is perfect for celebrating the original juicy fruit, the watermelon. It is carved a lot like a Halloween pumpkin, and is sure to brighten up your picnics. Makes 1 monster salad

- - - - - - - YOU WILL NEED - - - - - - -

- 1 large round watermelon
- Large knife
- Large metal spoon
- 2 large bowls
- 2 kiwis

- 1 cup strawberries
- 1 cup blueberries
- 1 banana, sliced
- Melon baller

- 1 cantaloupe, halved and seeds removed
- Pumpkin-carving tools or paring knife
- Toothpicks
- 1 lime

1 Roll the watermelon around on a cutting board to gauge how it stands best. This is how the fruit monster will sit.

2 Mark the approximate center of the front of the melon and, using a large knife, the supervising adult should cut a large mouth with pointy teeth. Use the knife in a sawing motion, and cut straight into the flesh of the watermelon at a 90-degree angle. Start with the center of the mouth and work your way outward. Remove the chunk of jagged mouth and set aside.

3 Use a large metal spoon through the mouth to scoop out as much of the watermelon flesh as you can. Scoop it into one of the large bowls and set aside.

4 Wash the kiwis, strawberries, and blueberries. An adult should cut the larger fruit into slices and chunks. Peel the kiwis and slice the strawberries. Using the melon baller, scoop balls from the reserved watermelon and cantaloupe. Place all of the cut fruit into the second large bowl. Add the blueberries and banana slices and toss gently to mix.

5 Lay the watermelon on its back to fill the mouth with the fruit salad. Carefully set it back upright so none of the fruit spills out.

6 Using the pumpkin-carving tools and toothpicks, create the rest of the monster's face. The lime, cut in half, makes superb eyes. Push a toothpick into each eye area and then push the lime halves onto the toothpicks so the cut halves are facing out. You can use more toothpicks poked into the cut limes to add banana irises and blueberry pupils.

THE AMAZING MUSHROOM WREATH

Fungi are amazing fun little guys. Make this mushroom wreath to let everyone know you are celebrating the amazing mushroom. Makes 1 wreath

YOU WILL NEED

- Scissors
- ½-yd-by-40-in piece Astroturf
- Gardening gloves
- 3 to 4 ft 22- to 24-gauge wire
- 9- to 12-in diameter hay or foam wreath
- Polymer clay
- Low-temperature glue gun
- Acrylic paint in the colors of your selected mushroom variety
- Paintbrush

1 First go to the library or sit down at the computer, and research mushrooms. Choose the type of mushroom you will make. With more than 38,000 varieties, there is a lot to choose from.

2 Using scissors, the supervising adult should cut the Astroturf into 3-by-40-inch strips. You will end up with 6 strips. Be sure to wear gloves and work out-side (or in an area that can be easily vacuumed), because cutting Astro-turf can be very messy.

3 Using scissors, cut the wire into 10-inch lengths. Push one piece of wire through the end of one strip of Astroturf. (Astroturf is a porous fabric so pushing the wire through it is like pushing a needle through fabric.) Wrap the long length of wire around the wreath and twist both ends together to secure and hold your first strip of Astroturf to the wreath. Begin to wrap the Astroturf strips around the wreath, starting with the first strip that you attached with wire, one by one, taking care to overlap each piece so that the wreath does not show through. When you get to the end of one strip, use one of the cut lengths of wire threaded through each strip to attach them together. Twist the wire together and cover the wire with Astroturf as you wrap.

continued . . .

4 When the wreath is completely covered, use wire to attach the end of the Astroturf to the first piece, making sure the wire is on the back side of the wreath. Twist the wire tightly.

5 Break off a small bit of clay and work with it in your hands until it is warm. Shape the clay into a mushroom stem and cap. Use a bit of the wire to poke a hole in the bottom of the stem. Repeat until you have made enough mushrooms for the wreath.

6 Bake the mushrooms according to the polymer clay manufacturer's instructions. Let cool.

7 On a covered work surface, use the low-temperature glue gun to attach 3-inch-long pieces of wire into the bottom of the mushrooms. Set aside to dry.

8 Using the paint and paintbrush, paint the mushrooms to resemble the mushroom variety you have chosen. (This is when all that research comes in handy.) Allow to dry completely.

9 Adhere the mushrooms to the wreath. Using the low-temperature glue gun, put a small bit of glue on the end of each wire and then push it into the wreath through the Astroturf. Once all the mushrooms are attached, hang the wreath on your front door.

HOMESPUN BOOKMARK

Today is the perfect excuse to take some time out to read a book. Reading is not only good fun, it's a wonderful hobby that encourages imagination and education. This beautiful bookmark is the perfect gift to help someone you love to remember to take time for reading every day. Makes 1 bookmark

YOU WILL NEED

- Ruler
- Pencil
- 4-by-8-in piece sturdy cardboard
- Scissors
- Tape
- Ball strong string
- Tapestry needle
- Lengths of yarn in various colors and patterns

1 Using a ruler and pencil, measure and mark ¼-inch increments across each of the short sides of the cardboard.

2 Using scissors, cut ¼-inch slits along the cardboard at the ¼-inch marks. You'll use these slits to form the warp—the vertical threads that form the base of the weaving.

3 Tape the end of the string to the back of the cardboard; placement does not matter—this is just to hold your string in place. Bring the rest of the string around front and, following diagrams a–e on page 116, thread the string up and down through the slits making

sure the string stays on the front of your cardboard loom. The only string on the back will be the loops in the slits.

4 Once you reach the end, cut the string and tape it to the back securely.

5 Thread the tapestry needle with your first piece of yarn.

6 With the first row, starting on the right side, move the needle over then under until you reach the end of that row. Make sure you leave a long tail outside the loom. When working with younger children, you may want to even tape the tail to the back of the board so

continued . . .

it doesn't get pulled through while they weave. When you finish the first row you will begin the second row, starting at the side you ended (the left side).

7 With the second row, starting on the left side, move the needle under then over until you reach the end of the row. Diagram f shows how these threads, called the weft, will create a woven fabric.

8 Whenever you come to the end of a piece of yarn, tie the next color to it, or leave a long tail to weave in later, when the bookmark is finished.

9 Repeat until the cardboard loom is filled with different colors of yarn. Leave a long tail of yarn to be tied into a knot with the fringe.

10 To create fringe, using scissors, cut twenty 4-inch-long pieces of yarn. Carefully remove the weaving from the loom, one loop at a time. Pass a piece of yarn through the loop and tie a knot, leaving the tails to form the fringe. Repeat until all of the loops have been finished with fringe.

11 Using the tapestry needle, carefully weave in any remaining yarn tails.

a.
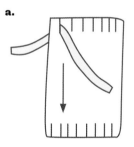

b.
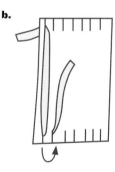

c.

d.
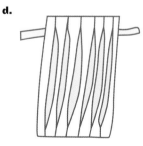

e.
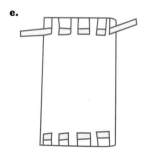

f.
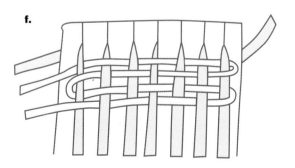

A DAPPER MR. PEANUT

NO ADULT NEEDED

This September take a break to celebrate the amazing peanut. Peanuts are actually not really nuts, they are part of the legume family, like green beans. These little peanut men are a cheerful way to honor this versatile and tasty treat. Crafting creatures and people out of peanuts was actually popular in the 1970s and you can sometimes come across peanut Santas, peanut butterflies, or little peanut flowers in thrift shops today. Makes 1 peanut man

YOU WILL NEED

- 1 peanut in shell
- Wooden skewer
- 2 pipe cleaners
- Scissors
- Black fine-point felt-tip pen
- Fabric scrap
- Tacky glue
- Tiny plastic top hat

1 Decide which part of your peanut will be the head and which will be the bottom. Using the wooden skewer, slowly poke holes for the arms to go through. The holes should go straight through the center of the shell. Use the skewer to poke two holes in the bottom for the legs. Leave sufficient space between the holes so the shell does not collapse.

2 Insert 1 pipe cleaner carefully into one arm hole and work it around until it comes out the other arm hole. Decide on arm length and, using scissors, trim the pipe cleaner as necessary.

3 Curve the tip of the remaining pipe cleaner slightly. Insert it slowly into one leg hole. Gently push it back down through the other leg hole. Decide on leg length and, using scissors, trim the pipe cleaner as necessary.

4 Bend the tip of each arm and leg slightly, to give the look of hands and feet.

5 Using the felt-tip pen, draw a face on the peanut. Experiment with different expressions: happy, sad, or scared on a scrap piece of paper before drawing on the peanut.

continued . . .

6 Using scissors, cut a small bow tie for the peanut from the scrap of fabric. Cut two triangles that meet up at one point.

7 Glue the bow tie on the peanut just below the face.

8 Apply a little ring of glue inside the bottom edge of the top hat and slide it down on to the peanut's head. Let dry.

9 If your peanut man is lonely, why not make more little peanut friends? You can make as many as you wish.

FALL LEAF-PRINTED NAPKINS

When most people think about fall and the changing of the seasons they envision leaves changing color and falling off the trees. Create these fall-inspired napkins no matter what the autumn months will bring to your region. All you need is some fabric paint and leaves. Makes 4 napkins

YOU WILL NEED

- Fresh leaves in various types and sizes
- Newspaper

- 4 white cotton napkins
- Your choice of fall-colored fabric paints

- Paintbrush
- Paper towels
- Brayer

NOTE

Gathering the fresh leaves for this project can make for a fun family outing. Go to the park, the forest, or your backyard and look for a variety of colors. If you're going into the wilderness or forest, read up on how to recognize poisonous plants before you set out. Various types of brayers, or hand ink rollers, are available at most craft shops.

1 Gather fresh leaves in various shapes and sizes. Look for leaves that are soft and pliable and avoid working with dry brittle leaves as they will crack and fall apart.

2 Cover your work space with newspaper. This will protect the area from the fabric paints.

3 Lay out a napkin flat on a sheet of the newspaper.

4 Choose your first leaf and apply a thin layer of fabric paint using the paintbrush. Coat the side with the most raised veins, to create a more attractive print.

continued . . .

5 Position the paint-covered leaf, paint side down, wherever you like on your napkin. Cover the leaf with a paper towel and, using even pressure, roll the brayer back and forth over the leaf several times. The paper towel helps prevent any fabric paint from getting on the brayer.

6 Repeat this process using various leaves and colors until your napkin is well covered. Set the napkin aside to dry for several hours.

7 Repeat the printing process until all napkins are covered. You can reuse leaves several times each.

8 Once the napkins are completely dry, an adult should heat-set the fabric paint according to instructions on the paint packaging. Most fabric paints are heat-set using a dryer or hot iron.

YOM
KIPPUR

10TH DAY OF THE
HEBREW MONTH
TISHRI, IN SEP
OR OCT

JONAH AND THE WHALE SUN CATCHER

YOM KIPPUR is a Jewish holiday also known as the Day of Atonement. It is one of the most widely observed holidays on the Jewish calendar. The day is traditionally observed with fasting, prayer, and spending the day in synagogue services. The story of Jonah and the whale is usually read during services. Making a sun catcher of Jonah inside the belly of a whale is a fun way to share this story with the kids. Makes 1 sun catcher

- - - YOU WILL NEED - - -

- Stack of newspapers
- Three 12-by-14-in sheets wax paper
- Crayon sharpener
- 3 or 4 blue, blue-green, and aqua crayons
- Towel
- Iron
- Black felt-tip marker
- One 2-by-3-in piece cardstock
- Scissors
- Hole punch
- Yarn or string for hanging

1 Lay out the newspapers to cover your workspace. You will want a nice thick stack of ten sheets or more. Lay one sheet of wax paper down on top of the stack.

2 Using the sharpener, sharpen all the crayons and let the shavings fall all over the wax paper.

3 The supervising adult should lay another piece of wax paper over the crayon shavings and cover with a towel. Using an iron on low heat, iron over the wax-paper layers. The crayons melt very easily, so you don't need to iron for more than a few seconds. Lift the towel and allow to cool completely.

continued . . .

4 While the crayon is cooling, let your child use the marker to draw Jonah on the cardstock. Use the scissors to cut him out.

5 Center the Jonah cutout over the top layer of wax paper. The supervising adult should lay the third sheet of wax paper and towel over Jonah and iron again on low heat to melt the wax of the wax paper so all three layers bond together. Iron quickly; it is okay if a little of the coloring comes through and turns Jonah a light shade of blue; this makes him appear to be inside the whale. If you want to avoid the blue, iron closely around Jonah, but not over the top of him. Let cool.

6 Let your child draw a whale onto the wax paper using the marker. They should draw the whale so Jonah appears in the middle. Use scissors to cut whale out.

7 Once the whale has been cut out, use the hole punch to punch a hole in the top and thread string or yarn through for hanging.

October

CUPCAKE CHAPEAUX

Throw a tea party in honor of the Hatter from Lewis Carroll's beloved book *Alice's Adventures in Wonderland*. These cupcakes look like little top hats and have "10/6" on the paper slip to match the illustration by John Tenniel in *Wonderland*. While 10/6 may have referred to the price of 10 shillings 6 pence, it also makes a wonderful date to celebrate. Makes 24 cupcakes

- **YOU WILL NEED** -

For the cupcakes:
- Mini muffin tin for 24 mini cupcakes
- 2 bowls; 1 large, 1 small
- 2 cups granulated sugar
- ½ cup nonhydrogenated shortening
- ¼ cup unsweetened cocoa powder
- 2 eggs
- 1 cup milk
- 1 tbsp distilled white vinegar
- 1 cup boiling water

- 1 tsp baking soda
- 2 cups flour
- 1½ tsp baking powder
- ½ tsp salt

For the ganache:
- 12 oz dark chocolate
- 2 tsp butter
- Large bowl
- Small saucepan
- 1½ cups heavy whipping cream
- Wire whisk

- Aluminum foil
- Wire rack
- Spoon
- Butter knife
- Baking sheet
- 24 packaged 3-in cookies
- Scissors
- One to two 8½-by-11-in sheets white cardstock
- Black fine-point felt-tip pen
- Sharp knife
- Red fruit roll-ups

 To make the cupcakes: Preheat an oven to 350°F. Grease the muffin tin.

 In the large bowl, cream the sugar and shortening until fluffy.

continued . . .

3 Add the cocoa and eggs and mix well.

4 In the small bowl combine the milk and vinegar and let sit for 5 to 10 minutes, until the milk appears to be curdled.

5 Meanwhile, pour the boiling water over the sugar mixture and let sit for 2 minutes.

6 Add the baking soda to the curdled milk mixture and then slowly stir the milk mixture into the sugar mixture.

7 While stirring, add the flour, baking powder, and salt and stir gently until well combined.

8 Pour the batter into the muffin cups, and bake in the oven for 10 to 15 minutes, until the cupcakes pull away from the side slightly. Remove from the oven and let cool completely.

9 To make the ganache: Chop the chocolate into small pieces. Place the chocolate and butter in the large bowl. Set aside.

10 In the saucepan, bring the cream to a light boil stirring constantly. Pour over the chocolate mixture and use the whisk to combine, whisking until the chocolate has melted and the mixture is smooth and pourable.

11 Place a sheet of aluminum foil under the rack to catch any spills. Remove the cupcakes from the tin and set on the rack. Carefully spoon a small amount of ganache over each cupcake to coat. Use a butter knife to coat the sides. Leave the bottom uncoated. If you would like to speed up the ganache-hardening process, put the rack with cupcakes in the refrigerator for an hour or so. You should have leftover ganache.

12 Once the ganache on the cupcakes has hardened, remove them from the rack onto a baking sheet. Place the cookies on the rack instead.

13 Reheat the ganache over low heat, stirring continuously, until the mixture is warmed and pourable.

14 Spoon a little ganache over each cookie. Using the butter knife, spread it out evenly. Top each cookie with one mini cupcake.

15 Transfer the hats to the refrigerator until completely set.

16 Meanwhile, using the photo on page 131 for inspiration, cut the 10/6 papers from the cardstock.

17 Using a felt-tip pen, write "10/6" on each piece of paper.

18 Using a sharp knife, cut the red fruit roll-ups into ¼-by-4-inch strips.

19 Remove the cupcakes from the refrigerator and gently press one paper to each cupcake. Secure it in place with one strip of fruit roll-up. The fruit roll-up will look like a hat band.

WALNUT-SHELL SAILING SHIP

COLUMBUS DAY is celebrated on the anniversary of Christopher Columbus's arrival in America. This holiday is one of the oldest American holidays dating back to the eighteenth century. Columbus Day also honors the heritage of the many Italian Americans. Indigenous People's Day is celebrated on the same day to recognize those who lived here before the arrival of Columbus. I think the history behind both are wonderful things to research with your children. My family has both English and Native American roots, each of which we believe are equally important parts of our past to explore and celebrate with our children. These mini ships use walnut shells for the hull. Black walnuts are native to North America and had been used by indigenous people for food and medicine. **Makes 1 ship**

- **YOU WILL NEED** -

- Scissors
- 2-in-square decorative paper

- Newspaper
- 1 walnut shell half
- Taper candle

- Matches
- Toothpick

1 Using scissors, cut two small slits in the paper, one at the top and one near the bottom, so it will easily slide onto the toothpick.

2 Cover your workspace with newspaper. Place the walnut shell, hollow side up, on the newspaper.

continued . . .

3 The supervising adult should light the candle with the matches and drip wax into the inside of the walnut shell. The wax should be deep enough to stand the toothpick in. Hold the toothpick in place until the wax hardens.

4 Slide the paper sail down onto the toothpick mast.

5 Bring your walnut ship outside and place it in a puddle. Blow the sail or wait for a breeze to move it along.

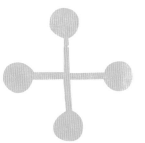

PEACE CRANE

Origami is a traditional Japanese art of folding paper. One sheet of paper is folded without the aid of glue or cutting to create intricate designs. One of the most recognized origami designs is the Japanese paper crane, also called the "peace crane." Using the same folding techniques but with fabric and liquid stiffener, you can create little origami gift baskets to celebrate the art. Makes 1 crane

YOU WILL NEED

- Liquid fabric stiffener
- 8-by-10-in shallow pan
- 12-in-square fabric in color or pattern of your choice
- Newspapers or towel
- Blow dryer (optional)
- Pencil
- X-Acto knife
- Hole punch
- 6-in 24-gauge wire
- Ribbon (optional)

NOTE

The larger the square of fabric you use, the easier it will be to fold. For small children or origami beginners you may want to cut larger squares of fabric, and let them practice the folding techniques on paper first.

1 Add a thin layer of the fabric stiffener to cover the bottom of the pan. Push the square of fabric down into the pan so the fabric stiffener coats it completely.

2 Let the fabric soak for a few minutes. Meanwhile, cover a workspace with newspapers.

3 Remove the fabric from the stiffener and lay flat on the covered newspapers. Use your hands to remove any excess of the fabric stiffener. Squeeze off any excess over the pan. The fabric should be wet, but not dripping.

4 While the fabric is still damp, follow diagrams a–k on page 138 and fold the

continued . . .

fabric into the shape of a paper crane. Follow the steps one at a time, allowing the fabric to dry a little between each step.

5 Prop up the head of the crane while it dries; you can set the crane down into a bowl, cardboard box, or another small container for drying. This helps the crane keep its shape and not fall flat. You can help speed up the drying process with help from a blow dryer, if you wish. As the fabric dries it will become stiff and frozen in position, so you will want to check on it frequently to make sure it is still holding the proper shape. Let dry completely before moving on to step 6.

6 Using a pencil, draw a small circle on the back of the crane. This is the area that will be cut away to make the crane into a basket.

7 The supervising adult should use the X-Acto blade to cut away this circle of fabric, using a sawing motion. Remove the fabric.

8 Using the hole punch, punch out two holes, one on the left side of the opening and one on the right, near the top edge.

9 Feed the wire through the holes and twist it around itself to form a handle. Now you can fill the basket with origami paper, instructions, or some origami shapes you have made, and give it to a friend. Or use a ribbon to hang it as a decorative basket.

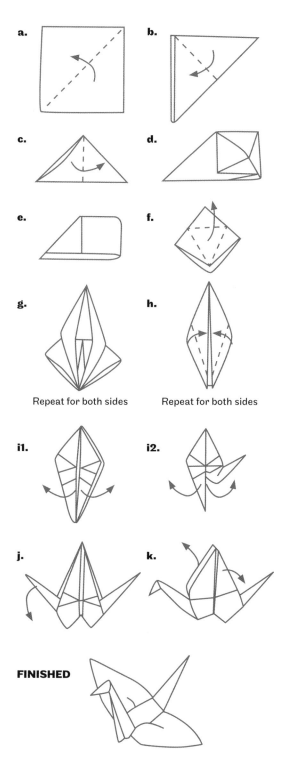

a.

b.

c.

d.

e.

f.

g.
Repeat for both sides

h.
Repeat for both sides

i1.

i2.

j.

k.

FINISHED

JACK-O'-LANTERN PILLOW

HALLOWEEN is a great time of year to carve pumpkins, tell spooky stories, and dress up in a costume for trick or treating. These pillow covers make great Halloween accents using pillows you already have around your house, and once the holiday is over, the covers come right off to be stored for next year. Makes 1 pillow

YOU WILL NEED

- 2 orange 100-percent wool sweaters
- 1 black 100-percent wool sweater
- Washing machine

- 1 tablespoon detergent
- Water soluble pen
- Scissors
- Dressmaker's chalk
- Pins

- Needle
- 1 skein black embroidery floss
- Sewing machine

NOTE

This is a great use for any wool sweaters that might be too small, riddled with holes, or just not worn anymore. Check thrift and second-hand shops for sweaters, too. If you are still unable to find a sweater that is 100-percent wool and orange, use the dye technique found on page 162 for the advent project to dye your own.

1 Cut the largest of your orange sweaters into a nice square shape. This involves cutting off the sleeves, sides, and back. Do not worry about your sweater fitting around your existing pillow just yet, because it is going to shrink when it is washed. Save the sleeves, sides, and extra pieces as those will be used to create the backing of your pillow. Leave the other orange and black sweaters whole as these will be cut after the felting process.

2 Felting is the process of matting the fibers in the wool into a thicker, sturdier fabric. This is done through agitation (in a washing macine) and with a little bit of detergent. Using the hottest temperature setting and the lowest water-level setting (if available) on your washer, place all the parts from your sweater and the whole sweaters into the washer. Add the detergent and turn on the washer.

continued . . .

3 When the washing cycle is done, pull the sweater pieces out. You will notice that the pieces have shrunk and become thicker. If any parts of your sweater look less felted, you can put them in the dryer for about ten minutes. Just keep checking on them so as not to over-felt.

4 Lay out the felted sweaters and sweater pieces to dry completely.

5 Take the uncut orange felted sweater and have your children draw a pumpkin onto the largest area of the sweater, using the water soluble pen. Using scissors, cut the pumpkin out and set aside.

6 Have your children draw a jack-o'-lantern's face on the felted black sweater using the dressmaker's chalk. Three triangles—two for the eyes and one for the nose work well—and a toothy grin for the mouth. Cut all the pieces out.

7 Using the pins, attach the pumpkin and face pieces onto the large square of felted sweater that is your pillow front.

8 Thread the needle with the black embroidery floss and use a blanket stitch (see page 86) to sew the pumpkin onto the pillow front. Sew on the face in the same manner.

9 If your felted jack-o'-lantern piece is much too small to cover the front of a pillow, add pieces from the sweater arms, sides, and back as needed to make the piece larger. Just cut thick strips and, using a sewing machine, sew them to the sides and back as needed to make the piece larger. You can also work with more then one sweater to have extra material.

If your sweater is larger then your pillow, that is okay. The sweater pieces should measure at least 1 inch bigger on all sides than your existing pillow. The measurements from now on will be for a standard 10-inch throw pillow.

10 Lay the 11-by-11-inch front (with the jack-o'-lantern), **Right** side up on a clean work surface.

11 Get your extra sweater pieces and cut two rectangles measuring 6 by 11 inches each. Lay these over the front side so that the edges are lined up, and the center edges overlap by 1 inch in the middle. Pin the sides together along the entire outside edge. You may also want to pin the back in place where the two fabrics overlap.

12 Using a sewing machine, sew around the entire outside edge leaving a ¼- to ½-inch seam allowance. Turn the pillow cover **Right** side out, through the opening where the two back sides overlap. Insert your pillow. You can also experiment with other colors. Try an all black pillow with a white appliqué ghost.

November

DAY OF THE DEAD

NOV 2

SKELETON COOKIES

EL DÍA DE LOS MUERTOS is a celebration for praying and remembering deceased loved ones. Some of the traditions include visiting the graves with gifts, creating sugar skulls, and building altars to honor beloved family and friends. It is a beautiful and colorful festival with flowers and parades intent on celebrating life. These gingerbread cookies might sound like something you would make for a winter holiday, but the use of royal icing turns these gingerbread boys, girls, and animals into skeletons instead. **Makes about 3 dozen cookies**

-------------------------------- **YOU WILL NEED** --------------------------------

- Baking sheet
- Parchment paper
- Large bowl
- 1/3 cup butter
- 1/3 cup nonhydrogenated shortening
- 3/4 cup brown sugar
- 2 tsp cinnamon
- 1 1/2 tsp ground ginger
- 3/4 tsp ground cloves
- 1/8 tsp black pepper

- 1/8 tsp ground cardamom
- 1/8 tsp ground coriander
- 1 1/2 tsp baking soda
- 1/2 tsp salt
- 2 1/2 cups all-purpose flour, plus more for dusting
- 1 tsp apple cider vinegar
- 1/4 to 1/3 cup water
- Rolling pin
- Cookie cutters in people and animal shapes

For the royal icing:
- Small bowl
- 1 cup confectioners' sugar
- 2 tsp milk
- 2 tsp light corn syrup, plus more as needed
- 1/4 tsp almond extract
- Resealable sandwich-size plastic bags, 1 for each person decorating

1 Cover the baking sheet with parchment paper. Preheat an oven to 375°F.

2 In a large bowl, cream the butter, shortening, and sugar until light and fluffy. Add all the spices and beat well.

continued . . .

3 Add the baking soda, salt, flour, vinegar, and just enough water to make smooth, pliable dough. Roll into a ball and chill for 30 minutes.

4 Press ball into a flat disc and, using a rolling pin, roll flat on a lightly floured piece of parchment paper to a $^3/_{16}$-inch thickness. Using cookie cutters, cut into shapes and transfer to the prepared baking sheet. Keep the uncooked dough in the refrigerator between baking.

5 Bake 7 to 10 minutes, until lightly browned. Remove from oven. Let cool completely.

6 To make the icing: In a small bowl, stir the confectioners' sugar and milk until smooth.

7 Beat in the corn syrup and almond extract until the icing has a smooth glossy consistency. If it is too thick, add a small amount of corn syrup until smooth.

8 Put the icing into resealable bags, one for each child helping with decorating.

9 Seal the bags and cut a small hole in one corner of each bag. Let your children pipe skeleton bones and skulls onto the cookies. You can research bones beforehand, or make them up as you go along.

10 Allow the cookies to set for several hours, until the royal icing is completely firm, and then store in an airtight container for up to one week.

RED-WHITE-AND-BLUE COOKIES

Presidential elections are held every four years. You can celebrate by baking these red-white-and-blue cookies into flags, election hats, or whatever election-related objects you like, then enjoy while you watch the votes come in.

Makes 12 to 15 cookies

YOU WILL NEED

- Baking sheet
- Parchment paper
- 5 bowls; 1 large, 1 medium, 3 small
- $3/4$ cup butter at room temperature
- 3 oz cream cheese at room temperature

- 1 cup granulated sugar
- 1 large egg
- 1 tsp vanilla
- $2^3/4$ cups all-purpose flour
- 1 tsp baking powder
- $1/4$ tsp salt

- Red and blue gel food coloring
- Disposable food-grade gloves (optional)
- Plastic wrap
- Wax paper

1 Cover a baking sheet with parchment paper.

2 In the large bowl cream the butter, cream cheese, and sugar until fluffy. Add the egg and vanilla and beat until smooth.

3 In the medium bowl sift the flour, baking powder, and salt. Add the dry ingredients to the wet ingredients and mix until a dough forms.

4 Divide the dough among the three small bowls. Add a small amount of food coloring to two of the bowls and knead until mixed in well. (For white dough, don't color the third bowl.) You may want to wear disposable food-grade gloves to knead, to prevent the food coloring from staining your hands.

5 Wrap all the dough pieces in separate pieces of plastic wrap and place in the refrigerator to chill for at least 2 hours.

continued . . .

6 When the dough is chilled and you are ready to bake the cookies, preheat an oven to 350°F.

7 Cover your workspace with wax paper and place each dough piece on top. Work with dough like you would Play-doh—create election flags, hats, and other election objects.

8 Place the cookies on the prepared baking sheet and bake for 8 minutes, or until the dough is just lightly browned. Remove from oven. Let cool completely. Store at room temperature in an airtight container for up to 1 week.

ROCK CANDY

Halloween may be over, but November 4 sneaks up to pay homage to all that dandy candy. Luckily the process of making rock candy is not only sweet, but scientific. So you're learning while you're eating. It helps, too, that it can take up to a week to form the sugar crystals, giving you plenty of time to make a dent in your candy stash before you indulge in this delicious treat. Makes 2 strings of candy

YOU WILL NEED

- Two 6-in lengths 100-percent cotton string
- 2 wooden skewers long enough to fit across the top of jar
- 2 glass jars or cups, 6-in tall or taller
- 2 cups water
- 2 cups granulated sugar plus extra for rolling string
- Saucepan
- Food coloring
- Plastic wrap

1 Tie the end of each length of cotton string into the center of each skewer, making sure it is firmly in place. Make sure the string does not touch the bottom of the jar when it hangs inside. If it does, cut the cotton string so it doesn't hang down so far.

2 Dip the string in water and roll it in granulated sugar while on the skewer. This will form a coating base for the sugar crystals to cling to as they form. Set this aside to dry.

3 The supervising adult should bring the water to a boil in a saucepan. Once the water is boiling, the adult should add the sugar 1 cup at a time, stirring constantly. Continue to stir until all the sugar has dissolved. The mixture should be clear and at a rolling boil before you remove it from heat.

4 Add 2 or 3 drops of food coloring to the sugar-water mixture, and then stir to mix in. Be careful; the mixture will be hot.

continued . . .

5 Allow the sugar mixture to cool for 15 minutes. Then the supervising adult should carefully pour the mixture into the two jars. The mixture will still be very hot and should be handled with care.

6 Slowly lower the string into the jars. Place the jars in a spot where they can sit undisturbed for up to a week. Cover the top of the jars loosely with plastic wrap so dust does not get in.

7 The sugar crystals will begin to grow after the first couple of hours. Let them grow for up to a week to form larger crystals; just make sure that the rock candy does not get so wide you can't pull it out of the mouth of the jar!

RECYCLED MINI ROBOT

Don't let the name of this holiday fool you. Though it may be an American holiday, it can and should be celebrated all over! Recycling is the process where used materials are turned into new products. Recycling centers turn plastic bags into park benches, and old newspapers into notebooks. Recycling is just one of the ways we can reduce our carbon footprint. Reduce and reuse are key parts as well. This project shows you how to turn used disposable materials into something new. Makes various robots

YOU WILL NEED

- Used cardboard boxes, toilet paper rolls, and other paper packaging
- Used tin cans

- Small used bits of plastic like empty thread spools, tape rolls or dispensers, and other items
- Low-temperature glue gun
- Scissors or cutting tool (optional)

- Newspapers
- Silver spray paint
- Tacky glue

NOTE Make it a family mission to gather used packages and small discarded items such as small cardboard boxes, plastic milk rings, bottle caps, and other items.

1 Look at your assembled recyclables and think about how you could use some of these to put together a mini robot. There are no rules on how a robot must look—they come in all shapes and sizes. Play around with your materials before doing any gluing.

2 The supervising adult should help with the glue gun, attaching the pieces of the robot. A small box can be the torso, and a toilet paper roll cut in half could become the legs, for example.

continued . . .

3 In a well-ventilated area, preferably outside, on a surface covered with old newspapers, the adult should spray the whole robot with a thin coat of spray paint. Let dry, and then spray the robot with another thin coat of spray paint. Let dry again. (Thin coats are preferable to thicker ones, because thicker coats will drip and take longer to dry.)

4 While the robot dries, figure out what materials to use for buttons and eyes. Colorful cereal boxes are great for buttons. You can find numbers and letters on most food boxes. Apply tacky glue to the items you have chosen for eyes and buttons. Let the small pieces dry before letting the kids play with their new robot.

TURKEY DAY GREETING CARD

NO ADULT NEEDED

Turkey has come to be recognized as a symbol of THANKSGIVING. Whether you eat turkey, or, like my family, enjoy a nice roasted Tofurkey, most people seem to associate turkeys with Thanksgiving. Traditionally, Thanksgiving is a holiday celebrated to give thanks for bountiful harvest, but nowadays most people gather with friends and family to express gratitude and thanks for the people in their lives. It is a time of sharing and letting those you love know you care. These turkey cards are great for sending to friends or family you might not be able to see, or would make wonderful invitations inviting your loved ones to share Thanksgiving with you. **Makes 1 card**

YOU WILL NEED

- Black fine-point felt-tip pen
- Brown blank card and envelope
- Tacky glue
- Two 8½-by-11-in sheets cardstock
- Orange and red glitter

 1 Using the felt-tip pen, let your child draw pictures of turkeys on the front of the card. While he or she is drawing, you can talk with your child about what Thanksgiving means to you and to him or her.

2 Apply a thin line of glue along the outlines of the legs and beak in your child's drawing.

3 Lay the card on the sheet of cardstock. Let your child sprinkle the orange glitter over it. Gently lift the card and shake any extra glitter off onto the cardstock. Set aside to dry.

4 Apply a thin line of glue along the outlines of the body and feathers of the turkey.

 5 Lay the card on the second sheet of cardstock. Let your child sprinkle the red glitter over it. Gently lift the card and shake any extra glitter off onto the cardstock. Set aside to dry.

 6 Let the card dry completely before writing inside and mailing.

December

ADVENT CALENDAR FOREST

In our family, the start of December means the start of an ADVENT calendar. We use it to count down the days until Christmas, and add a little happy surprise to each day. Advent calendars can be used to count down to any upcoming family celebration. This little forest of Advent trees makes use of old sweaters that are felted to stand easily. (Prizes hidden underneath include small trinkets, candy, and little love notes telling the finder how much they mean to you.) Makes 1 calendar

------------------------------ **YOU WILL NEED** ------------------------------

- 1 large or 2 small green (or white, off-white, or cream) 100-percent wool sweaters
- 3 or 4 packets green unsweetened Kool-Aid per sweater (optional; only if using light-colored sweaters)
- Washing machine

- 1 tbsp detergent
- Scissors
- Pins
- 12 pipe cleaners, cut in half
- Needle or sewing machine
- Green thread to match sweater
- Pencil (optional)
- Iron

- ¾-yd-by-40-in fusible webbing
- ½-yd-by-40-in brown felt
- ⅛-yd-by-40-in cotton contrasting fabric
- Tailor's chalk (optional)
- 24 small treats or trinkets plus optional decorations

NOTE

This is a great use for any wool sweaters that might be too small, riddled with holes, or just not worn anymore. Check thrift and secondhand shops for old 100-percent wool sweaters. If you are still unable to find green sweaters that are 100-percent wool, look for sweaters that are white, off-white, cream, or yellow and dye them, following the instructions on page 162. In this project, you will use the felting technique. Felting is the process of matting the wool fibers into a thicker, sturdier fabric by machine washing them in hot water.

continued . . .

1 If you do not have a green sweater, dye a white, off-white, or cream one. Take a large bucket and fill it with 1 to 2 gallons of hot water. Add the Kool-Aid and stir until completely dissolved. Submerge the sweater and allow to sit in the mixture until the water looks fairly clear. (The citric acid in the Kool-Aid sets the dye so it will not bleed.) Rinse the sweater in the sink until the water runs clear. Repeat if using more than 1 sweater.

2 Using the hottest temperature setting and the lowest water-level setting (if available) on your washer, place the sweater into the washer. Add the detergent and turn on the washer.

3 When the washing cycle is done, pull the sweater out. You will notice that it has shrunk and become thicker. If any parts of the sweater look less felted, you can put them in the dryer for about 10 minutes, checking every few minutes so as not to over-felt.

4 Lay out the felted pieces to dry completely.

5 Using the template on page 188 as a guide, use scissors to cut out trees from the sweaters. If you are counting down to Christmas you will need to cut out 24 trees.

6 Fold the tree pieces in half lengthwise, so that the two edges are lined up. Pin along the edges to hold them together. Insert a pipe cleaner into each top between the fold, positioned so 1 inch is hidden inside the tree and 1 inch sticks out the top.

7 Using the needle or a sewing machine and matching thread, sew over the pipe cleaner in each tree several times to secure, and bend the end of the pipe cleaner right below where it is sewn to help keep it in place. Turn each tree **Right** side out. These are fairly easy to turn right side out; if you have any trouble with the tips you can use the eraser end of a pencil to help get out the top points. Each should have a 1-inch length of pipe cleaner sticking out of the top.

8 The supervising adult should iron the ½-yd-by-40 inches of fusible webbing onto the brown felt. Using scissors, cut the pinecones from the brown felt using the template on page 188 as a guide. The pinecones will be an oval shape without any snips. Cut the fusible webbing to size. Each pinecone should have two pieces, and each should have fusible webbing on one side.

9 Starting with one tree, place one pinecone piece, fusible webbing side up, on a clean work surface. Lay the pipe cleaner at the top of the tree on top of it, so that the base of the pinecone touches the top of the tree. Place another pinecone piece, fusible webbing side down, on top, sandwiching the pipe cleaner in the middle. The adult should carefully iron the pinecone sandwich on both sides to secure the webbing. (Alternatively, you could use glue instead of fusible webbing to secure the pinecones; just make sure you let it dry for several hours before going any further.) Using scissors, make small, downward snips along the sides of the ovals for the spiky edges of the pinecones.

10 The adult should iron the remaining fusible webbing onto the back of the cotton fabric. You or your child can draw the numbers 1 through 24 backwards onto the paper side of fusible webbing. Alternatively, just draw directly onto the front of the fabric using tailor's chalk.

11 Using scissors, cut out the numbers and arrange them on the pinecones. Peel the paper backing off the fusible webbing and lay them on the pinecones. The adult should iron them to adhere to the cones.

12 Your advent forest is now complete. Arrange the trees on a table or mantle as a decoration, adding real pinecones if you wish, and maybe some little plastic deer.

13 Add a treat or trinket underneath each cone so that the treat is hidden underneath, and begin your countdown. One tree is lifted each day to reveal the hidden treat underneath.

ST. LUCIA'S CROWN OF LIGHT

ST. LUCIA DAY is an important holiday in Scandinavia. It is a festival of light, and marks the beginning of the Christmas season for people in Scandinavian countries. To celebrate, a female member of the family plays the role of St. Lucia by dressing in white and wearing a crown of candles. Everyone in your family can celebrate with a crown of candles made from paper using a technique called *quilling*. Makes 1 crown

YOU WILL NEED

- Scissors
- 1 sheet 9-by-12-in red construction paper
- 1 sheet 9-by-12-in yellow construction paper
- Ruler
- Toothpick
- Tacky glue
- 3 or 4 sheets 9-by-12-in white construction paper
- 18 to 24 rubber bands
- Tape measure
- 3 or 4 sheets 9-by-12-in green construction paper
- Pencil
- Clothespins
- Low-temperature glue gun
- Stapler

NOTE

Quilling is the art of rolling thin strips of paper into various shapes, and then using these shapes to create a design.
For this project, the candles' flames will be made by quilling.

 1 Using scissors, cut the red and yellow paper into ⅛-by-12-inch strips. For younger children, cut the strips wider to make the rolling easier.

2 Take one strip of red paper, moisten one end of the ⅛-inch side with water, and stick it to the toothpick. Then begin to wind the paper around and around the toothpick until the

continued . . .

strip is completely wound up and tightly coiled. Gently pull the toothpick out and with your hand press down any of the paper that pulled out from the coil when you removed the toothpick. Place a small dab of glue on the end of the paper and press down to finish the coil. Repeat, making 6 to 8 coils, depending on how many candles you desire for the crown. Let dry completely.

3 Using the glue, adhere the short end of a yellow strip of paper to the red flame center. Begin loosely rolling the yellow strip around the center but pinch at the top each time to form a crease. When you get to the end of the yellow strip, glue it down in place. Repeat, covering the remaining red flame centers. Let dry completely.

4 Using scissors, cut one sheet white construction paper in half lengthwise, to make two long, thin rectangles. Roll one of the rectangles tightly lengthwise. When you reach the end, place a line of glue along the edge, and press down to finish the roll. Then lay this candle down on the second rectangle of white paper and roll again, finishing in the same way

with the line of glue. Wrap 3 rubber bands around the candle to hold it in place as it dries. Repeat, making 6 to 8 candles.

5 Using a tape measure, determine the circumference of your child's head. Using scissors, cut the green construction paper into a 2-inch-wide strip whose length equals your child's head circumference plus 2 inches. Using a pencil, mark a 1-inch-long area at each end.

6 Cut additional green construction paper into strips, each 4 by 2 inches. You will need 1 strip for each candle. Using dabs of glue, adhere each candle to the crown, equidistant from each other. Do not glue any candles in the 1-inch overlap area at the ends.

7 Coat the green strips with glue and press them lengthwise onto each lower portion of candle. The strip should wrap around the candle and press down on both sides onto the crown. This will ensure that the candles stay glued in place. Use clothespins on each side of the candles to hold the strips in place on the crown as they dry. Let dry completely.

8 Using the quilling technique, make as many three-dimensional leaves as you would like. You can use various shades of green. Take one strip of green paper, moisten one end of the ⅛-inch side with water, and stick it to the toothpick. Then begin to wind the paper around and around the toothpick until the strip is completely wound up and tightly coiled. Gently pull the toothpick out and with your hand press down any of the paper that pulled out from the coil when you removed the toothpick. Place a small dab of glue on the end of the paper and press down to finish the coil. Repeat, making 6 to 8 coils, depending on how many leaves you desire for the crown. Let dry completely. Using the glue, adhere the short end of a green strip of paper to the green leaf center. Begin loosely rolling the second green strip around the center but pinch at the top each time to form a crease. When you get to the end of the strip, glue it down in place. Repeat, covering the remaining green leaf centers. Let dry completely.

9 Cut out 1- to 2-inch two-dimensional leaf shapes from green construction paper as well.

10 Using a low-temperature glue gun, adhere the flames to the top of each candle with small dabs of glue. Using the glue gun, adhere the leaves along the crown with small dabs of glue.

11 Overlap the ends of your crown so the two pencil lines meet up. Staple the two ends together near the top and bottom, and wear.

GLITTERY MINI MENORAH

NO ADULT NEEDED

HANUKKAH is also known as the "festival of lights." It is a celebration that commemorates the Jews' victory over the Greeks more then 2,000 years ago. Each evening at sundown the Hanukkah menorah is lit. The menorah is a specialized candle holder with nine braches for nine candles. The middle candle, the Shamash, is used to light the other eight. Create a very special mini menorah that is just the right size for kids. Always have an adult help with lighting. Makes 1 menorah

----- YOU WILL NEED -----

● 6 oz Paperclay   ● 1 tbsp glitter   ● 9 birthday cake candles

1 Work the Paperclay with your hands until soft. Add the glitter and mix until the glitter is mixed in well.

2 Shape the clay into a rectangular shape at least 5 inches long.

3 Use one of the candle bottoms to create 9 holes across the top of your clay menorah. Try to make the holes at least 2 inches deep. Allow the menorah to dry for several hours or overnight.

4 Once the menorah is dry, insert all 9 candles. The candles should fit snugly.

5 On the first night, the candle to the far right is lit, and on the second night the second candle to the right, and so on until the eighth night when all eight candles are lit.

WOODLAND GNOME

WINTER SOLSTICE is the shortest day of the year in the Northern Hemisphere and marks the first true day of winter. Using some bits from nature and a little bit of felt, you can create these little winter gnomes to celebrate. Makes 1 gnome

YOU WILL NEED

- Scissors
- Felt scraps in colors of your choice
- Tacky glue or low-temperature glue gun
- Small pinecone
- Toothpick
- White acrylic paint
- Black and red fine-point felt-tip pens
- Acorn

1 Using scissors, cut the gnome's hat and feet from the felt scraps. Cut into triangles measuring 2 inches tall and 1½ inches wide at the base.

2 Apply glue to the bottom of the pinecone and press the feet onto it. Let dry.

3 Roll the hat piece into a pointy cone shape and glue the two straight edges together. If you are using tacky glue, make a line of glue that runs down the long edge of the hat, and hold the hat edges in place for a few minutes before setting down, to allow the felt time to really adhere; if you are using a glue gun, it will dry very quickly. Let dry.

4 Use a toothpick dipped in white paint, and create two eyes on each gnome. Once the white paint is dry, create the pupils with the black felt-tip pen. Using the black felt-tip pen, draw a smile. Using the red pen, color in rosy cheeks and a nose.

5 Apply glue to the top of the pinecone and press the acorn head onto the pinecone body. When the glue is set, apply glue to the top of the head and press the bottom edge of the hat to the top of the gnome head. Let dry completely.

6 If the gnome is feeling lonesome, make him some woodland friends using more pinecones and different colors of felt or other fabric for their hats.

GINGERBREAD HOUSE TISSUE-BOX COZY

One of my family's favorite traditions each CHRISTMAS is creating a gingerbread house. Here's one you can create that will last year after year. You can experiment with all sorts of little bits and bobs to create a truly unique house.

Makes 1 cozy

YOU WILL NEED

- Scissors
- ¼-yd-by-40-in brown felt, plus scraps in various colors
- Pins
- Embroidery needle
- Embroidery floss
- 5 ¼-by-4 ¼-by-4 ¼-in box of facial tissue
- Tacky glue
- Buttons, beads, and any baubles that resemble candy

NOTE

You can use buttons, beads, rickrack, yarn, pom-poms, glitter, and wiggly eyes as decorations. Or make your own faux candies by wrapping small pom-poms in colorful tissue paper and twisting the ends. These will look like real candy and, once glued in place, will stayed wrapped.

1 Using scissors, cut out all of the pieces from the brown felt using the diagram on page 174 and the facial tissue box as a guide. Lay the pieces out flat on a clean work surface.

2 Pin all of the chimney pieces in place. Using the embroidery needle and floss, sew up the sides of the chimney with a blanket stitch (see page 86). Work your stitches from left to right. Begin by bringing your needle to the outer edge of the fabric at point A. Insert your needle back into the fabric at point B. Push your thread through both fabrics in a straight line so it is coming out at point C. Your thread should be behind the needle as it goes through the fabric. Continue to stitch taking note that point C now becomes point A for the next stitch. The thread will form a nice edging around the fabric. Finish off with a knot and clip threads.

continued . . .

Pin the body of the gingerbread house together and sew the pieces together with a blanket stitch.

 Pin the chimney in place onto the house and sew it on using a backstitch (see page 20).

 To decorate your house, pull it over the tissue box to stabilize it. If you want to add stitching as decoration around the windows and doors, do so now. You can use various colors of embroidery floss and various stitches to create designs.

 Apply small dabs of glue to the box and attach bits and baubles, just as you would with a real gingerbread house. Let dry completely.

 Pull tissue up through the chimney to create "smoke." Pull a tissue from the chimney whenever you need one.

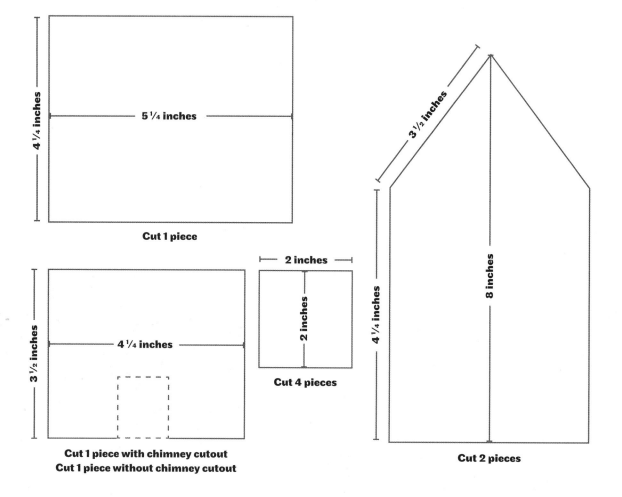

4 ¼ inches

5 ¼ inches

Cut 1 piece

3 ½ inches

4 ¼ inches

Cut 1 piece with chimney cutout
Cut 1 piece without chimney cutout

2 inches

2 inches

Cut 4 pieces

3 ½ inches

4 ¼ inches

8 inches

Cut 2 pieces

Packaging
&Wrapping

FOOD BOXES

So many holidays involve making and baking food for people we love. These easy-to-make boxes (pictured on page 175) look like gingerbread houses and make a perfect takeaway container for food gifts or Christmas cookie boxes. In the summer you can fill them with mini loaves of zucchini bread made from your garden. The blank gable boxes come in many colors and sizes, but I like the small brown boxes for this project.

YOU WILL NEED

- White opaque paint pen
- Brown paper bags (optional)
- Small cardboard gable boxes, available at paper and packaging supply stores
- Wax paper

1 Review the paint pen instructions from the manufacturer to get the flow of ink started. Let your children practice using the pen on brown paper bags first.

2 Using the paint pen, draw a simple door and windows on the front and sides of the box. Draw staggered scalloped lines or other design on the slanted sides of the box to make the roof.

3 Using pieces of wax paper, line the inside of the box before putting in your treats. This will keep any oil from staining the box.

4 Fill with goodies and give away!

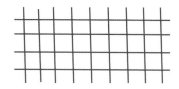

MONSTER GIFT BOX

A monster gift box is perfect for gifts that might have an awkward shape difficult to wrap in paper. You can slide gifts inside these monsters made from empty cardboard food boxes. The best part is that they can be reused over and over, and not just for gifts.

YOU WILL NEED

- Glue
- Small cereal, cracker, or other food box
- String or large rubber band (optional)
- Spray paint in color of your choice
- Newspapers
- Ruler
- Pencil
- X-Acto knife
- Scissors
- Felt scraps
- Self-adhesive Velcro
- Faux fur or pom-poms
- Wiggly eyes (optional)
- Button or bamble for nose (optional)

1 Apply glue to the underside of the top opening of the box and press it closed, so the box looks like a new, unopened box of food. You can help hold it in place with string or a very large rubber band. Let dry.

2 In a well-ventilated area, preferably outside, on a surface covered with old newspapers, the supervising adult should spray the whole box with spray paint. Let dry, and then spray the box in another thin coat of spray paint. Let dry completely before moving to step 3.

3 Use the ruler and pencil to create the new cutting lines for opening the box. Measure and mark 2 inches down from the top on each of the narrow sides of the box. Using ruler and pencil, draw a diagonal line from the upper left corner of the box down to the 2-inch line. Repeat on the other side of the box, but with the diagonal line from the upper right corner.

4 Using ruler and pencil, measure down 2 inches from the top on the front of the box, and draw a line across the front.

continued . . .

5 The adult should use an X-Acto blade to cut the diagonal side lines and front straight line. This will form a new opening for the box—the monster's mouth.

6 Open the mouth. Using scissors, cut teeth for your monster from felt. Glue the teeth onto the inside of the box where the mouth opens. The teeth should hang down so that they overlap the bottom half of the mouth. Let dry.

7 Once the teeth are dry, attach one side of the Velcro to the back of the teeth and the other side to the lower mouth. The Velcro and teeth should line up so that to open the gift, you lift its teeth and the upper part of the monster's mouth.

8 Now you can decorate your monster. Apply glue to the top of the box and attach bits of faux fur or pom-poms for hair. Apply glue and attach wiggly eyes and nose directly on to the cardboard box. The monster can be as elaborate or plain as you would like it to be.

CREATING BOWS

Bows can create a finished look to the top of any gift, but store-bought bows are often impractical, impersonal, and can be a waste of money. Turn your children's drawings into beautiful bows that will not only be very special, but easy to use again and again.

- YOU WILL NEED - - - - - - - - - - - - - - - - - - -

- Drawing paper
- Crayons, markers, or paint
- Scissors
- Glue
- 5 clothespins

1 Let your children draw and decorate the paper using crayons, markers, or paint. If they would rather do small drawings that you will be able to see on the ribbon, cut the ribbon first before they decorate it. Big abstract drawings and paintings also make beautiful bows.

2 Using scissors, cut the paper into ½-inch strips. The strips do not need to be very long—6 inches or so will work fine. The most important thing is that all the strips for each bow are the same length.

continued . . .

3 Each bow will need 4 strips of paper. Place a strip of paper facedown on a clean work surface and put a drop of glue in the center (see diagram a). Bring one end of the bow toward the center dot of glue and press the **Right** side of the paper onto the glue, thus creating a loop (see diagram b). Put another drop of glue in the center and bring the other end of the bow toward the center. This time come from the reverse side, and again press the **Right** side of the paper down onto the glue. Use a clothespin to hold the papers in place. Your bow should look a little like the number 8 (see diagram c).

4 Repeat with the next 3 strips of paper, holding the centers of each with a clothespin until they dry.

5 Take half of a strip and make a circle, gluing it so the **Right** side of the drawing is on the outside. Hold it in place with a clothespin.

6 Once all the bow layers are dry, assemble them. Lay the first bow layer down so the drawing side is facedown. Add a drop of glue to the center and lay another bow layer on top of it, facedown as well.

7 Glue the final loop in place on top. Let dry completely. Position it on top of a gift by running ribbon through the bow instead of taping it in place. This way it can be reused again and again.

a.

b.

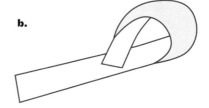

c.

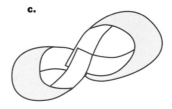

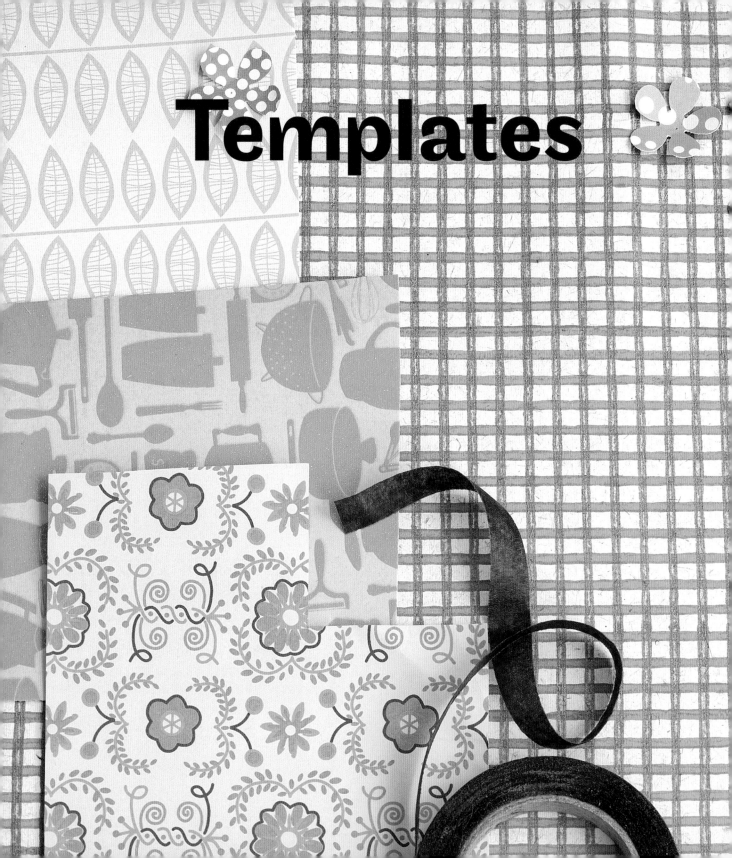

Templates

**Punxsutawney Phil
Shadow Puppet**

Viva La Piñata!—mouth

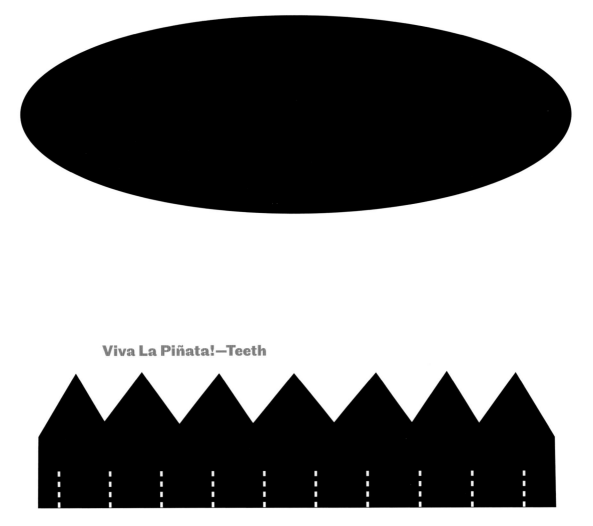

Viva La Piñata!—Teeth

Felted Love Bugs

Sparkly Bunnies

A Poppy for Remembrance

Canadian Flag Garland

**Love Your Mother Earth
Tote Bag**

Advent Calendar Forest—Tree

Advent Calendar Forest—Pinecone

every day's a holiday :: **188**

Resources List

Whenever possible I recommend supporting small independently owned shops and businesses.

~~~~~~

General Art Supplies & Adhesives

* AC Moore
www.acmoore.com

* Dick Blick
www.dickblick.com

* Flax Art
www.flaxart.com

* Michaels
www.michaels.com

Paper

* Creative Papers
www.handmade-paper.us

* Paper Source
www.paper-source.com

Fabric & Felt

* Prairie Point Junction
www.prairiepointjunction.com

* Purl Patchwork
www.purlsoho.com

* Reprodepot
www.reprodepot.com

* Sew Mama Sew
www.sewmamasew.com

* Superbuzzy
www.superbuzzy.com

Cake Supplies & Sprinkles

* Bake It Pretty
www.bakeitpretty.com

* Fancy Flours
www.fancyflours.com

Embroidery

* ABC Stitch
www.abcstitch.com

* Cecilia's Samplers
www.ceciliassamplers.com

Wooden Parts

* AC Moore
www.acmoore.com

* Hobby Lobby
www.hobbylobby.com

* Michaels
www.michaels.com

Wool Roving & Yarn

* The Felted Ewe
www.thefeltedewe.com

* Spinster Yarns and Fibers
Spinsteryarnsandfibers.com

Vegetable Glycerin

* Frontier Co-op
www.frontiercoop.com

* Star West Botanicals
www.starwest-botanicals.com

More Inspiration

* Craft Zine
www.craftzine.com

* The Crafty Crow
www.belladia.typepad.com/crafty_crow

* Crafty Pod
www.craftypod.com

* DIY Kids
www.d-i-y-kids.blogspot.com

* Scrumdilly Do
www.scrumdillydo.blogspot.com

Index